The Day of Fire

What is this World?

by David Stewart

The Day of Fire: What is this World?
Copyright © 2018 by David Stewart

All rights reserved. No part of this work may be used or reproduced in any manner without written permission except in brief quotations.

Published in the Unites States by
  Seek Find Books
  Warrenton, VA
  6008 Jaclyn Drive

ISBN: 978-0-9996755-0-2
E-book ISBN: 978-0-9996755-1-9

Cover Image by Nageen Asif
Cover Design by C5 Designs

Printed in the United States of America

Contents

Fire	1
Things Internal	21
The Decision	35
Anger	51
We do not Understand	67
We Want Certainty	75
Lost in the Universe	83
Certainty in Science & Philosophy	97
How Could We Find Certain Answers in Religion	109
Does Reason Exist?	117
Gödel's Theorem	125
The Limits of Reason	135
The Other Way	155
Conclusion on Knowing, Understanding, and Feeling	169
Happiness, the Elusive	175
End-all of Happiness	191
Conclusion of My Life, and of Fulfillment	207
The Best Answer	223

Fire

I want to say in beginning that I would not have considered this story to be worth putting on paper and would have spared the world yet another book, if it hadn't been for the event that happened to me on July 4th, 1996. Some of the description below might still be tedious to read, or may seem pretentious, but I've included all of the background as well as I could in order to put the events in context.

I was a good natured child to start with, and I was happy. I can remember picking little bundles of twigs, grass, and flowers from the yard and tying them together with a string to give to my mother. And I remember that I didn't like to see anyone else unhappy. I was very caring and good.

When I got to be about eight I wasn't those things anymore. People will debate the question of when children become accountable for what they do, and not many would consider that age to be eight years old, but when I think back about what I started out as, and what I became, it's clear that, that was the time. That was when I turned proud and selfish, and the change happened suddenly in me.

My affections dried up as well, and even as a child in second grade I was known for showing no emotion and for doing bad things. None of my teachers in elementary school liked me, and I can see now that they had good reason. I was the best at a lot of things then, and I knew it, and that did not benefit what was being formed inside me; for the same reason that a lot of women who are the most attractive on the outside are the very ugliest people inside. Pride ruins people, the damage that it does goes deep, and it's somewhere between hard and impossible to undo it later on. So there were no more bunches of grass and flowers for my mother anymore, and not much thought for anyone but myself.

I had an easy time in early childhood, then, but things flipped to the complete opposite in middle school when I began to feel more clearly what kind of person I was. To help give a sufficient context, I'll mention that I was a pretty tough boy in some ways. I played every game for years in a row on a competitive team, for example—fall, spring, summer, and winter—whether I was hurt or not, even with injuries like the ones I can still feel in my ankle and hip more than twenty years later. However, with my first year of middle school began crushing anxiety every waking moment; so much that I could, quite literally, barely speak. A fear of some people also began, as did a feeling of worthlessness. I was tread on occasionally and I came to be regarded by both other people and by myself for what I actually was inside—nothing. I can promise that there is no pain quite like that. I didn't ever think of suicide, but I did think that it would have been better for me to be dead, and I came to the point of wishing for that.

I won't try to wring words out to describe just how bad that period was for me, but it was enough to be something I could never forget, and something that will always be a part of me. However, a lot of people never get the correction that I got during those years. They will never learn the truth about themselves, and never be chastened deeply enough in this world to bring about any change. So I'm thankful now that it all happened to me. Anything less intense or painful probably would not have done what it ended up helping to do.

Things got a lot better in high school during my second year. I was able to stand a little more upright by then and not to think as badly of myself, which made the pain decrease. For context, I was 6'1", about 170 my third year, and I had a couple friends that were in agreement with me that the best thing in life was to get messed up as much and as often as possible. We smoked weed all the time and hung out in the driveway drinking every weekend, and I played a sport at school. So things looked fairly normal on the outside. But I'd never had more than a couple friends, I did not get along, barely spoke, always kept to myself, was still hurting, and I did not like a lot of the things I saw in people or the way life was. There are happy kids that nothing seems to bother, and who don't seem to go through any pain. I'm glad for that; but I certainly wasn't one of them.

In the beginning of my third year of high school, though, for some reason, a change started inside me that ended up being the most important thing that's ever happened to me, and the only great thing I've ever been a part of. It was made of two elements. The first one was a desire to become somebody that I could live with. A lot of young men will have that particular drive, and some of them will also put their very best effort into it. It's part of development, and I'm not the only person who has learned that it's hard to live with yourself if there's nothing inside of you that's worth anything. The aspect of this drive in me, though, that was out of the ordinary was that I became determined not just to settle at some point on the spectrum of personal worth where I could feel alright about myself. I became willing to keep going to the very bitter end of that course of achieving value, and of trying to become what we should all truly be, according to the conclusions of logic.

The second part of the change was an effort to find out the truth about life. It quickly came to mean everything to me to find out whether there was a God and whether there was any existence for us after death. I *had* to know. I thought about it all the time, and by the end of that year I was in quite a place. Whatever answers I found to those questions were going to determine everything for me:

what I would do, how I would feel, and possibly whether I would continue on with even the appearance of any normal kind of life.

There was no event that caused that shift to begin in me—although there was a definite dividing line of before and after, near the beginning of that year. The things that happened are also hard to describe since almost all of it took place strictly within my own head. One of the elements that made up the change was intellectual—seeking truth. The other was moral—striving to become something worthy. But part of the difficulty in describing what happened comes because the intellectual and the moral parts of human beings are intertwined. I have found that what we *are* inside will affect what we are able to see and to appreciate with our minds. It's a strange truth, but those who don't have much value inside themselves simply will not be able to appreciate the importance of anything in life, and they will not be able to see clearly.

Previous to the year of these changes I had always been that kind of person—whose sight and voice meant nothing. But soon after the year began, I made decisions that planted something in me and allowed me to pick my head up and see. Among the things I saw for the first time was a very clear view of what I, or any other person, should be, and to see that, if there was a God, the only thing that mattered was to do what was right. That was, and is, very obvious logically. I realized that, regardless of whether a person cares about good or not, the truth is that if they don't try to do what's right, they are not only immoral, they are simply stupid. No one disputes that our life on earth is nothing compared to eternity, so our happiness here counts nothing compared to our happiness in eternity, if there is one for us. And I saw that after our life here is over, what we did here and what we were like here is what will matter, if anything will. Someone who is honest and who does what's right doesn't have to have been born sickeningly good, or even care about what's right; he just has to be *logical*.

Those facts became very clear to me, and they really aren't hard to figure out. What made them unusual and worth mentioning in my case, though, was that I didn't just see it and nod and then go on just like I had before. I decided to follow the conclusions entirely, and all the way to the end, as anyone who has a properly functioning brain would. That's the one aspect of it that was a little bit admirable—that I made a decision like an adult to actually make myself do what had been decided, and to do what was right, always, no matter what.

Element One

So a change had begun. The kind of dispassionate decision I just described happened early on, and it was some of the motivation for that change, but my own feelings also played a role when I began to look inward. When I turned my gaze around to look at myself, what I saw there affected me deeply. I'll mention an exceptional example to illustrate this, because those examples can be communicated most clearly, but I should say that the same issues are at stake in regular boring experience, and what was evident in this one anecdote wasn't limited to it in any way, but it extended into everything.

As I began to spend time in silent thought that year, the memory of one event that had happened the previous school year stood out in my mind and demonstrated an unpleasant fact to me. A guy that I was not friends with, but usually talked with in one class, and had gone to the same elementary school with, got into a problem with a rough group of kids. One of the individuals in that group that I knew of probably would have killed somebody, depending, and there actually was an issue with a gun at least once while I was at the school. Everyone knew who they were. Some kids who tried to act like this type were laughable, but these were not. The guy that I talked with in the class hadn't done anything, and they knew it, but they wanted to see a fight and to throw weight around.

His name was Jason, he was scared, and he came by and asked me one day at lunch, "Do you have my back?" I didn't tell him that I did. I did nothing. Very few people would have, but when I reflected back on it, that comparison to other people didn't matter to me. Whatever I might have said, the fact was that I was not someone who was worth enough to stand up for anything either way. As I sat in my room the next year and thought about this event, and all the other situations like it in life that call for something inside that I had never shown, and had never had, I was ashamed. Beginning that year, for the first time in my life, I became ashamed of what I had done, what I had been, and what I had not been.

And, no, I didn't watch Jason get beaten half to death and just stand there. There wasn't a fight at all in the end. But, again, one particular situation is not what this reflection on myself was about. The feelings that started taking life inside me had to do with the thing I had come to see at the bottom of my failures in general, which was cowardice and worthlessness, stinking and yellow.

I can remember realizing what I had always been in life, and what I would leave as always and forever having been David Stewart after I was gone from this world. And I could see that when I died and it was all over—which I thought about very seriously, very often—that disgrace was what I would be leaving. And this realization made something burn inside me.

However, I decided that I would no longer be a disgrace. And I would never do anything shameful again. So help me. I made this resolution and, within a short time afterwards, just the possibility that I might find myself in some other situation and not be enough of a genuine entity to do what I should do, etched a resolve deeply into me. "*Never again*" I said to myself. "I would rather die." And I was serious enough to die over it, or over anything like it, as far as I was capable. So, something resembling an actual man was born right there, and a big part of the change in me happened there, with that decision.

In summary, then, because of these new feelings I had, and because of the logical conclusions that had become so clear to me about what we should do in this world—in case there is an eternity for us—I determined that I would always do what was right. As hard to believe as it might be, especially for someone who had known me, I resolved that if I ever saw cruelty taking place in front of me, or any other situation that called for some kind of action or sacrifice, whatever it might be, I would do what I *should* do. Something that might make that easier to believe, though, is the fact that my motivation in this was for *me*; because it was what *I* wanted for myself. Also, I had not changed so that I loved and cared about people, but I had certainly changed so that I hated cowardice and hated things that weren't right.

I should also try to emphasize that this decision, and the intensity of it, was very far from normal. Today if I think about something like my failures and about situations I might find myself in where I'm called on to act, I'm fairly determined that I'll try my best to do what I should. But my face doesn't heat up and I'm not ready to swear an oath on my soul, and to despise and destroy myself if I should not be able to act properly. Back during that year, I was. If I had failed then, and done what I had sworn I never would again, it would have been just about time for ritual suicide for me. I was probably as serious and idealistic as only a very young person could be, and as committed as only someone who had experienced a bad enough taste of life could be.

Follow-through

So, the decision was made, the commitment was there, and the objective was obviously right—scary or not, feeling or no feeling. But I found that the problem with the whole thing, and with trying to live it out, was that it was also difficult; bordering on impossible. This was especially true since I was working with someone, in myself, who was weak and fearful by nature. I realized that I would probably have to be a lot stronger and a lot more fearless than I actually was if I was going to be able to live up to my new principles. For that reason I set to work on myself to become, basically, an extension of my decisions.

Taking a course like this with a complete commitment was like casting off from shore and leaving myself. And while that might sound romantic, it was difficult and uncomfortable, like leaving a familiar home to live exposed on a sheet of rock. The overall goal was good, and the soundness of the conclusions I had made gave me resolve to continue, but it was hard enough to keep on this path of becoming someone who could *always* do what he should, that I didn't want anything holding me back if I could separate myself from it. So I deliberately tried to remove any attachments from myself. And this was not done out of malice, but because I honestly expected that continuing would mean my possible death, or something similarly frightening or difficult happening that I would have to be able to handle. And attachments don't help someone to face those things.

So, for one thing, I barely spoke to my mother anymore. I had not been her little boy for a long time before, so this new behavior—which I am not proud of as I have thought of it since—was not part of growing up, and it was something far from ordinary. It's part of any mother's job description to do all they can to grasp onto their sons and keep them under their wing, whether they're five or fifty. But that wasn't funny to me then. I remember her coming into my room once near the end of that year crying, saying she didn't know me anymore. I was sitting on a bench by the window and I said in a dead kind of voice that she was right, she didn't know me anymore. I have never been deliberately cruel, but that reply was necessary. I was gone and I wasn't coming back. And I was no kid, and it was no kid's running away from home game I was playing. I have never been as serious about anything again in my life, and I could never deal with anything more serious. It was the truth of all of existence, and it was me being committed to making myself into an extension of that truth. David had to be cut off and left behind for good.

Although I was, and am, weak, one thing that I did had to my advantage from the start in being able to pursue this course was that I wasn't enamored with life. (Misery helps a lot with that.) In a way I had felt better over the year when these changes took place because I could think decently of myself and could taste a little bit of freedom. But I was still far from enjoying my time, and I was still always suffering from anxiety, which by itself can cause someone to want to take drastic action of some sort—to throw life back maybe and say "if this is it, I don't want it." That constant problem of anxiety, by the way, was also a lot of the reason for me wanting to get zipped off to somewhere else by drugs all the time.

Also in my favor for having a willingness to cut all ties to normalcy or safety was that I had still never forgotten those earlier days, just a few years before, when I had felt the unique and intense pain of being something I couldn't live with and, again, of literally being barely able to speak from anxiety. That memory, which was still fresh within me, along with my state during the year of these changes, helped to make me willing to give everything up. So, despite the immense difficulty of it, to me it was good riddance to David, and to life.

Also on the topic of the deliberate separation I was creating, I can mention at least one other fact that took place in the physical world rather than just in my head. Although I was a year ahead in math, and was in the advanced English, I had deliberately not done a bit of work in school that year. I hadn't been overly concerned with schoolwork before then, but that year I stopped completely. The world's message about school, or about anything else that a good and wise person was supposed to do, was maybe that if he did it things would be okay and life would turn out well. That was the unspoken guidance from the guarding institution, from any adult, and from society. But I could not help remembering what I might have to be able to make myself do if certain things happened. I couldn't forget that it would be very far from alright with me if I was not able to do what I had sworn, but that it might be very far from alright for me physically if I *was* able to do it.

I realized very well that forcing the frail vessel of myself to stand up to all possible situations could mean some very violent events happening. And, as unlikely as it would be to encounter a situation that would cost my life, I had to be a person who would not fail if that situation happened either. And *yet*, I was supposed to be concerned with *school?* I remember, in trigonometry in particular, having my head on the desk every day trying to sleep—as in all my classes—and not doing one homework assignment all year, on principle. I remember once in that class hearing about an upcoming test and actually wanting to do something to prepare, but deliberately refusing to. I barely passed the course with a "D" and should have failed.

Generally, then, and overall, I kicked and dragged myself along to follow the logical course every step of the way to its correct end. Thinking back over things now, I can see that I had experienced enough discomfort in previous years that some kind of unusual reaction might have been expected. Maybe purple hair, or rings and crap stuck through my face. But as I've reflected later on I've recognized that none of the change that actually happened came as a result of any of my experience, and it certainly didn't come naturally as a matter of course, or as a result of growing up. I mentioned before that during that year when I changed, I spent time in silence, reflecting. But I should add that this was not just a few minutes on occasion. Throughout that year I spent up to hours *every day* sitting in my room thinking: about whether there was a God, about whether we are really just animals, about what I might have to do and that I swore that I would do. And I was renewing a resolution that I would not stop. Time seems to be the prerequisite to move forward in anything difficult, or to build resolution, and I can say that contemplating our own brief lives and the fact of our coming death can provide quite an education.

To finish describing this first element I'll repeat, as the most important thing, that I was serious about making myself do every single thing that lined up with principle, and not doing anything that didn't—unto death, and far beyond any comfort or mercy. I'll also say something of a type that normally would not be spoken by a subject about himself: I very rarely use this word, but what happened over that time was *special*. It's the only thing I've ever done in life that was, and I have hoped to somehow convey a little bit of the truth of that fact in order to communicate the story from beginning to end.

Element 2

The determination on what I would be was one half of the trek and the change. The other half was finding out the truth about this life. And I was similarly determined in that pursuit.

Before this year I had never seriously thought about whether there was a God, or about where human beings go when we die, but at the beginning of the school year I began asking myself those questions. Within a short time I insisted that I wouldn't go on in life without finding out. Also within a short time, I arrived at the conclusion that there probably was not a God. And the thing that made that conclusion consequential for me, whereas it means nothing for other people who say they believe it, was that it was not just a passing notion that I didn't care about. I planned to take whatever answer I found to heart, and to act accordingly; all the way.

I tried to understand what it would really mean if God didn't exist, and I was able to accomplish that goal without much trouble. Like the other realizations, it isn't hard to figure out, and it is one thing that can be described easily. If God didn't exist, I knew that it meant that there *is* no such thing as right or wrong, and that we are essentially no different from bacteria, or from any other kind of matter. I knew that if there is not a God, then we are atoms and the random tendencies holding them together, and nothing more. I knew that without God there is nothing right or wrong for humans any more than there would be for bacteria.

I also knew that, if God doesn't exist, there is no "meaning," and a child dying means no more than a single cell organism dying, or a chemical bond disintegrating. A person's pain wouldn't matter, like his happiness wouldn't matter, and just like nothing else that ever happened to him or to anyone or anything in this world would matter if there is not a God. I saw that feelings and ideas about morals and happiness and optimism would all be delusion; made up of arrangements of particles in the brain, and that sense organs to determine "pain," and cranial structures capable of producing an emotion, would be nothing but accidental groups of matter arranged in a particular way which, in turn, were equally likely to exist or not to exist, and would be equally meaningless either way. I realized that this is all we would be, and I internalized it all very deeply.

I understood back then also that people who say "there is no God," but then just go happily along with their lives, have no idea what it means. If those people truly understood their beliefs, and they were willing to accept the real implications, I knew that almost every one of them would change their stance pretty quickly, or they would try to hide their eyes from it and forget what they'd seen, because *nothing* could be more terrible.

At age seventeen I realized the simple implications very well and I felt just how dark it all was: no Father and no one looking out for you. No meaning. No such thing as love. Nothing. Accident. And no one can comfort you for that, and no one can make anything alright, ever, no matter what may be said. It would mean the end of any hope in life forever. Absolute darkness.

I took those things very, very deeply to heart and I knew that this hopelessness and meaninglessness was the bare truth of it — as it's apparent from some literature and from some suicides that others have as well. Nevertheless, I didn't ask for comfort from anyone. No one could change the truth, or what it meant, and I was determined to face reality without trying to go back and hide. I still never once actually thought about suicide, but, as for most people who do kill themselves, I also didn't whisper a word about my plans or about what was going on inside me to anyone else. Until the very end, I never considered talking to anyone else; both because I did not want to be comforted for something for which any comfort would be delusion, and because I did not want to hear a single word from someone who had obviously never thought about it, and who obviously didn't care about finding out.[1]

By the end of that year I wanted badly for God to exist, but I honestly did not think that he did. Based on what I was sure of, and based on the way life was, it looked to me like the possibility was probably just a hopeful and naïve wish. That was my very sincere conclusion—*there was no God*. Who can fit the meaning of that into their head? I had a good family and a normal type of background to start with in life, but that didn't matter anymore. I wasn't coming back to hide.

---

[1] There was a history for me in that lack of regard for the thoughts of others as well, since I had never been told what was true about God or death by my family, or by society. I will mention, though, that, in the way of education, the one piece of religious knowledge I had been informed of by my elders was that all life had evolved out of some kind of scum in the ocean. That was taught as a fact, I regarded it that way, and the important thing about this was that I was able and willing to put two and two together to see what that origin of life really implied about existence overall, and about what we are. I described that picture above.

Most of our life is internal, and the paths that we take are inside us. That's where the most important things are. I didn't go anywhere physically during that year, and most people couldn't see anything happening on the outside, but I went a very long distance inside myself and something had definitely happened there. Taking a broad look at the circumstances I've described also evokes one question in particular to me: *What kid in high school, with my history especially, is determined to live by any moral principle, or insists on finding ultimate answers about life?* It's only logical to do any of those things for one's own future, and, again, I personally did it for my*self*, and because it was what *I* wanted. But it was also exceptionally rare. It simply does not happen.

In childhood I'd been one of the strongest, the quickest with my mouth, and had been known for doing things that shouldn't be done. "Who put the rubber band on the projector light bulb?" "Probably David Stewart." "Who broke out the windows?" David Stewart. "Who stuffed the sweatshirt in the toilet?" David Stewart. And who was bad to other children, was completely selfish, and had no courage or anything upstanding in him? I did, and was. Then, later, in adolescence, the ugly nature of what I was became apparent to me, and I felt the pain of that fact very intensely inside. But then, just a couple years after that, I was doing something truly noble, and had become someone who was truly worth something. Somehow, and amazingly, that happened.

In reflection I can also say that I do my duty in life now, and that I can force myself to stand up when someone has to, but when I think back about that year I know that I was easily more of a man then, at seventeen, problems and all, than I ever have been since, or will be again. Today I am also still very serious by nature, but I have never been so serious about anything again. The conviction about what I would do, and what I would not ever do, was burning at quite a temperature, and I was going to find out the truth about life and God no matter what it would mean—hopelessness, my own death, some other kind of life, or anything that was called for. I will always be more proud of this fact than of anything else I've ever done.

In the end, though, I knew that I couldn't keep up that kind of life and striving—it was just too difficult. But I also wouldn't stop. So I did realize that something had to give. And, fortunately, it did.

The end

This was my third year of high school, and by the following summer I was at about the end as it turned out. It finally became a possibility to me then to try to find out if someone else might know some answers, and there was one guy on my soccer team that demonstrated some kind of genuine belief, although, I didn't know what it was. I decided to talk to him. At the end of practice on July third, 1996 we sat on the field talking until the rest of the team had left, then I said what I wanted to get to, "*I don't think there is a God.*" He grabbed some dirt in his hand and said, "You couldn't have this without God." I will never forget that. It's still bright and indelible in my mind, as all my memories from that time are.

After a couple more words we sat in my car and talked for three hours. I voiced every argument against God that I could think of, not daring to let myself hope that he might exist. By the end of our conversation, though, I knew that I was wrong and that God *did* exist. There was no hoping or wishing or superstitious-man-animal myths about it; it was a fact and I knew it for certain. And it was beyond strange that I gained that kind of assurance from this conversation, because my teammate didn't give any brilliant, unheard of evidence that I hadn't considered before. Nevertheless, I somehow knew with complete certainty that there was a God. And that knowledge put me in some kind of state.

After we finished talking in the car I thought about the fact of God all day and night, and I was in a kind of shock, or prolonged amazement. I've experienced some other unforgettable things since that day as well, but I've never been in quite that kind of condition again, and I didn't get one second of sleep that night because of it. Always before when I couldn't sleep, I would at least doze off by 5 AM or some similar hour for a little while. But that night I did not sleep, doze off, or wander for one second into sleep or anything close to it, because I knew there was a God.

For quite a few years I haven't told anyone what exactly happened the next day, which, coincidentally, was the fourth of July. I did tell it several times after the event, but I eventually just got a bad feeling about it and began simply stating one or two facts, if anything. I still don't tell anyone in person, but I don't have such reservations about sharing it in writing. Putting the story down is actually most of the reason that I went to extensive lengths to be sure I got this book written.

The day after I talked to my friend in the car I went to DC with my brother and several of our friends for the 4th of July. A little while after we got where we were going and sat down, I started seeing a dark glowing red in everyone's eyes, and I knew that what I was seeing was the thing that I had hated and had tried my best not to commit for the past year. It was the ugliness I'd come to be able to perceive, and that I had said earlier was at the heart of the examples of failures I gave in my behavior and in that of other people.

It's difficult to describe the feeling I had after seeing this. It wasn't so much fear as it was exposure to something extremely big. I knew that I was seeing the bare truth, and all I could do was to keep on seeing and wait for whatever was coming next. So I sat with my friends for a while on the grass next to the Washington Monument where we had set up for the day, and I decided within several minutes that I had to get away on my own. I was still somehow concerned enough with manners to tell them I was leaving, and said the first excuse that came to mind—that I had soccer practice that day and had to go. One friend said, of course, "What are you talking about? It's the fourth of July." I sat back down and, that moment, two men walked just behind where I was sitting, one of them carrying a soccer ball. I said I was going to play with them and I got up and left.

I caught up to them and we exchanged a couple words as the three of us walked. We stopped by the northeast side of the monument at an open spot. I don't know why I didn't leave right then, but there was nothing that I could have done really. I didn't know what to do with what I was seeing, or what was happening to me, or what to say, so I asked them if they wanted to play. Stranger still, they replied, "No. We can't do that." A few seconds later, with the three of us still standing there, I said, "Can I see the ball?" and they repeated, "No. We can't do that."

After a couple more seconds one of them laid a gold colored blanket down on the ground, then I looked around to my right towards the monument. When I looked back to my left towards them, the place where he had put the blanket down was a window in the ground made of solid fire. I knew what it was, and what it meant, and I was terrified and I walked away without a word. As I left I heard one of them say to the other, "I think he saw something."

For the rest of the day I wandered around the mall near the monument and somehow kept seeing myself fail in all the things that I had sworn over the previous year that I would never do again. I can't describe how I saw that, but it was clear. At that point I also knew there *was* a God, and I had just seen that there is also justice for what's done in this world. I knew I would be in those flames, but I just could not keep from failing.

I never even asked myself if it was all really happening or if it was really true, because it just could not be denied. I couldn't have shielded my eyes from it even if I had wanted to. So I was placed directly in front of it all, and I had no hope, and I was in extreme distress and pain like I've never experienced before or since, but I had also had a lot of practice facing reality by that time and I had been a very serious person for a while before this. As it happened, I had been in very genuine training for the last year; imposed on myself by myself. And if it hadn't been for what had happened throughout that previous year I think I would have just curled up entirely that day, and simply would not have been able to see these things.

I stayed on the DC Mall all the way to the fireworks, but didn't watch them, then I took the Metro home. When I got home at about twelve at night I picked up a Bible my brother had and started reading the first gospel. I believed in Jesus Christ immediately when I saw his name in the first paragraph, and the terror was gone. I knew right away that he had saved me, without even having to read any further. I finished the first few pages and went to sleep.

The next day when I woke up I ate something then went out the front door. As I was standing in the driveway it occurred to me—also with a degree of certainty that I have almost never had again—that everyone on this earth is still here only because of God's grace. It definitely doesn't seem like that to me now usually, but I saw it then in some higher way. Then I went back to my room, finished reading *Matthew*, and decided to commit my whole life to God because I wanted to know him and to do what he wanted me to in life.

Later that night, just a few moments after I'd lied down to go to sleep, I started thinking again about the things I'd done, and how I had failed. I had done what had *disgusted* me and that I had sworn I never would again. And I started weeping—the first time I'd shed more than about one tear for years, as young men learn to do. Then in my mind I said two words, "forgive me." Immediately, then, I knew that God did forgive me, and my emotions flipped from grief to joy.

It was strange that over all the days and hours I had spent during the previous year thinking, and after all the effort I'd put into finding out what was true, the Bible had never even crossed my mind as a possibility. But now *I* was a Christian. Who would believe that.

I've looked back on that day a lot of times and wondered if it really happened. There have been a lot of things seen and claimed and ultimately found wrong or delusional in this world. But I've never panicked in my life, I've never had a mental illness, I've never hallucinated, everybody that knows me recognizes that I'm stable, I don't jump to conclusions, and I still doubt most things as being God's will or God's doing—more than any other Christian that I'm acquainted with. I'm very skeptical of things that people say God has done, and I consider most people to be truly naïve and superstitious about what is natural and what is genuinely divine action.

If anyone can doubt, analyze, or change his mind, that is also definitely me, and I have seriously doubted all of it many times since it happened. It didn't take long either. A few days after that July 4th, the dishes came crashing down and I wondered if it was all true. Anything is truly possible and there is very little that can be proved. However, every time I look back on things, it's still pretty hard to deny that some very strange circumstances and events lined up.

That day didn't just come out of nowhere. I still can't put my finger on anything during the months leading up to it and say "God did this." But I realize now that over the year leading up to July 4th, 1996, I had been trying to be *perfect* morally; although I never thought of it that way then. I tried with all the strength I could possibly find to do that, only to learn in the end that I was very far from being capable of it, no matter how committed to it I was. Throughout that time I had also said with all of my mind and with my life, "I want to know, and I'll face whatever it means!" And it looks suspiciously as though God heard me, and that he reached down directly to me saying, *"This is what's true. You asked for the truth, and this is it."* Also, by the way, everything I learned over July 3rd and 4th—before I had ever even read the Bible, or heard about it from anyone—was exactly in line with the biblical message of salvation.

So evidence indicates that I might very well not be a wacko, and that there probably actually is a personal God who reached down and delivered a vision of the truth of this existence to me. I will still add, though, that my beliefs don't hinge on my experience. If I found out that aliens had implanted fake memories of my entire youth, or that I was schizophrenic, etc., I would still believe the same things. And I know that it would not have taken the events of that day for me to believe the Bible. I was very sincere and I did not deny anything that I was convinced to be true out of personal motivations. And, from the first time I read it, I somehow knew that the biblical message of Jesus Christ as God and Savior was true.

That year was the most important time of my life, and that day was the most important event of my life. Sometimes, though, as when I wrote these things just now, I remember the feeling of terror and the thoughts of realizing an undeniable, "yes, it is happening, and you are seeing it, and this is the truth about everything." I would never want to go through anything like it again—not the year leading up to it, and especially not that day.

Things Internal

I'd like to mention at this point that I haven't assumed the truth of any one belief system in this book, except in a couple sections where I make note of that. I am convinced of the truth, but skepticism has a lot going for it, or, more accurately, fallibilism does—that humans do not possess certainty. More on those issues of certainty and doubt will be discussed later, but right now I think it's necessary to point out something about the way we think in western society. People with a scientific and materialistic background, such as myself and most Americans, can't hear certain things very well without having some balance applied to their mindset, so I want to present something about the way we think before going any further.

If there is a God that chose to create this existence, he would have to be an emotional being. A god that was emotionless would never create anything, since there wouldn't have been anything to motivate it. That god would have no desire for sharing life, or even for entertainment, since the ability to be entertained indicates some form of enjoyment; which is also a feeling or emotion. And emotionless god would also have no desire to make anything for the sake of beauty or goodness, since, without emotion, there would be no such thing as "good" and there would be no desire at all except maybe a lifeless survival instinct like bacteria have, determined by particles and physical forces.

Likewise, there could be no meaning to any human experience if people were incapable of feeling. Someone without feeling could win a state championship or get married, but he couldn't be even a little bit happy about those things, and he couldn't feel a sense of accomplishment, or anything else. Or, if he ended up living on the street eating garbage instead, that would mean as little to him as his former success might have meant. It wouldn't be any "better" or "worse" since those words would have no relevance without the existence of feeling. Anything that happened to an emotionless person would be equally dead. Even a child being born wouldn't matter.

In *War and Peace* Tolstoy gave a good description of what a person who could not feel would be like. In the passage, the character, Prince Andrei, had been badly wounded but was on his way to recovering until one night he had a dream in which he died. In the dream, Death forced open a door that Andrei was trying to close and lock, and Andrei woke up alive physically, but dead inside. His sister, son, and fiancee, were able to find him after Moscow had been burned and everyone was fleeing. But nothing had meaning for him anymore. When his sister arrived she asked,

> "But how is his wound? What condition is he in generally?"
> "You...you'll see," was all Natasha could say...two days ago," Natasha began, "*this* suddenly happened..." She suppressed her sobs. "I don't know, but you'll see how he's become."
> "He's grown weaker? thinner?..." asked the princess.
> "No, not that, but worse. You'll see..."
> There was almost hostility in that deep gaze, looking not out of but into himself, as he slowly examined his sister and Natasha. If he had shrieked in a desperate voice, that shriek would have terrified Princess Marya less than the sound of that voice.
> "And you've brought Nikolushka?"

> He said just as flatly and slowly, and with an obvious effort of recollection...She understood what had happened to him in those two days. In his words, in his tone, especially in that gaze—a cold, almost hostile gaze—there could be felt an alienation from everything of this world that was frightening in a living man. He clearly had difficulty now in understanding anything living..."Yes, they say it's burned down," he said. "That's a great pity," and he began to look straight ahead, absentmindedly stroking his mustache with his fingers.[2]

That is how life would be without feeling.

In this existence we live in, or in any existence that could even be conceived of, there would be no life if there was no feeling. Similarly, the existence of any thing would be completely devoid of meaning on its own without someone capable of feeling to see it or to eventually be affected by it. A galaxy could pop into existence or an earthquake could wreck an entire island, but without some living, feeling thing to be affected by those events, they wouldn't be good, bad, or otherwise; they would just be.

I don't think any evidence beyond just a couple thoughts should be required to demonstrate the truth of any of this. Discussions of this issue could grow to thousands of pages, but there's no need for that. One philosopher, David Berlinski, addresses the issue briefly,

> Within mathematical physics, things move dissectively *downward* toward the fundamental objects and their fundamental properties and laws. The universe thus revealed is *meaningless*, its fundamental laws controlling a vast but sterile and inaccessible arena...meaning is alien to

---

[2] Leo Tolstoy, *War and Peace*, Volume 4, part 1, chapter 15.

> physics...meaning appears only in the reflective and interpretive gaze of human beings.[3]

Meaning only exists "in the reflective and interpretive gaze of human beings" and it only exists there if we have the capacity for feeling. Without those things there is a computer, not a human being, and meaning vanishes, along with life.

What this means is that, in a way, feelings are everything—the heart is everything. It means that what we are inside is more important than any proof, discovery, scientific truth, or physical law, and that our heart is just as real. And the reason that I've begun the book by making this point is that this idea is contrary to the mindset of the Enlightenment, modernism, and rationalism, which is the age and attitude we were all born into and that we live in right now. And, no one with a rationalistic mindset would be able to hear some of the things that are communicated later unless some balance is introduced. The goal of this chapter is to provide some of that balance.

We too are in the stream of human history

People have been on the earth for a long time but, for the most part, we do not have access to a perspective spanning generations, and we don't realize what part of the river of time and history we're in, or what the attitude of our time is. There are changes in the spirit of the times, though, as centuries go by, and humanity's view of things really is different from what it was even a few hundred years ago.

Somewhere along the line there was a substantial shift in the way people, in the west at least, see and experience life. The Enlightenment is usually considered to have begun around 1690, but whenever the change toward scientific analysis and empiricism

---

[3] David Berlinski, *The Advent of the Algorithm* (San Diego: Harcourt Inc., 2000), 256.

started, and whatever it's called, before it there was superstition and ignorance, and afterwards there was scientific discovery and reasoned religious thought, or no religion at all. With The Enlightenment came death to voodoo medicine, good luck charms, subjugation to ignorant religious teaching, and the belief that titles made certain people gods on earth. Good riddance. But some other changes that were not so positive also entered into the human experience of life, and into our ability to recognize truths that can't be measured with a ruler or dissected under a microscope.[4]

The concept that feeling is more important than reason, or that it is just as real, would only have been stating what seemed obvious to anyone in mankind's history before logic became master of all. But to modern western people, (us) that thought seems surprising, and maybe even ridiculous. The mindset of rationalism—our current one—is definitely that feelings don't matter, the spiritual doesn't matter, personal experience of this life doesn't matter, and that probably, to be honest, none of those things are even real to start with; they're only pleasant delusions that comfort the human animal brain material. Western society has concluded that only the superstitious would believe any of the spiritual, feeling-type things, and we've attempted to stretch the methods and attitudes of the physical sciences to cover all of existence. This has caused an emphasis on corporeal objects and a

---

[4] One part of the change that isn't as commonly recognized was the shift in our regard for the inner life. Arthur Zajonc points out that this change is hinted at in the way that art changed with the Renaissance (Arthur Zajonc, *Catching the Light: The Entwined History of Light and Mind* (New York: Oxford University Press, 1993), 61). Ancient and pre-renaissance paintings are terrible as far as being accurate depictions of the physical. To our eyes it seems that people just couldn't paint for hundreds of years. Some of this could have been simple lack of skill, but what's more important was that, in their mindset, the physical was not as important as the feelings within us, or as important as spiritual truth. Things that were more valuable to people were painted bigger and placed in the foreground, for example, even if that made the painting incorrect geometrically. But, in later paintings, the internal had to make way for things external and physical after they had become more important in our eyes.

denial of the inner life. According to this worldview, the only things that exist are logical or empirical (they can be seen or measured). And anything that can't be seen or measured isn't real, or, at least, it isn't important.

One fairly colorful example illustrating the conflicting mindsets of before and after was in the movie *Master and Commander*. At one point the superstitious crew believed that one of the ensigns on their ship was cursed. They were living in the beginning of The Age of Reason, and the ship's doctor was surprised when he discerned that the captain, who was supposed to be an educated man, also believed there was a curse. The doctor confronted him about this, but instead of denying such an embarrassing naïeveté as would be expected, the captain said, "Not everything is in your books Stephen." But we disagree! We usually believe that *everything is* in our books, which are reasoned thought and the material universe encompassed by it. We are undoubtedly still in the age of logic now, and the associated attitudes have affected our thinking for quite a few generations.

No one would deny that the way we view the world changed with the Enlightenment, or that we are still a rationalistic people today. So none of these conclusions are going out on a limb. One professor says, for example, that anthropologists studying the US describe that Americans "tend to see the universe as a great machine constructed and operating under purely rational laws" and that we "are also given to pragmatic empiricism; that is, our test of the rightness of any course of action is whether it seems to work, to produce desirable results." Americans are empiricists, and this professor says that empiricism is the kind of thinking that insists on measuring and quantifying everything. If something can't be dealt with in this way, we're likely to discount it.[5]

---

[5] Lauren King, *The Way You Believe* (Newberg, Oregon: The Barclay Press, 1991), 63.

The theologian John Westerhoff makes another note on how our mindset affects us: "The current bankruptcy in our spiritual lives is not solely a misplaced singular concern for the intellectual way of thinking and knowing, but rather it is an actual denial and neglect of the intuitional way of thinking and knowing."[6] And Berlinski states that

> the deepest metaphysical assumptions that the physical sciences make, [are] assumptions that have themselves passed directly into the life of popular culture. The world, the physical sciences affirm almost with one harassing voice, is physical and not spiritual, numinous, or mental.[7]

Science was the driving force for rationalism, it is concerned with the empirical and nothing else, and that attitude has gotten into the population at large. That fact can be safely concluded. So, people who must quantify all things, who discount anything that can't be measured, who neglect the intuitional way of thinking, and who instinctually assume that the feeling and spiritual things don't matter... those people are *us*! That is how we think.

Just a brief look at the public schools demonstrates this. Art is cut, music is cut, there isn't even a course in ethics or any area like it, and very few people care about that neglect. However, math and science are valued highly and pushed constantly. I don't know if I've ever heard a political address where a speaker lamented the loss of artistic or philosophical ability in our kids, or said that we are really losing an appreciation for ethics. But doom is always predicted if we don't get better at math and the physical sciences. Our country is going down fast if we don't do that.

---

[6] John Westerhoff, Spiritual Life: The Foundation for Preaching and Teaching (Louisville: Westminster John Knox Press, 1994), 20.

[7] Berlinski, 277.

Politicians know what people want to hear and what they value—their jobs depend on it—so, obviously, what people value and want to hear is how we're going to get better at logic, and they do not value performance in areas involving emotion and inner life. I cannot see how the message there, starting with the population and then echoing back to us from the leaders, is not equal to this: "Things that have application in the physical world matter. What's inside you—feelings and your spirit—do not." That seems to be exactly what the message is to students, and that is what our society believes, although no one would say it straight out, and most wouldn't even recognize it consciously. If that was otherwise, the importance that we place on what kids should learn wouldn't be so lopsided. This particular focus (and neglect) in education is just one indicator of what we really believe, like a slip of the tongue, spilling the beans.[8]

I personally don't care that students should be able to play the recorder better or paint nicer pictures, but our attitudes that we take into life *do* matter, and the impact of those attitudes extend into the entire experience of each individual—*life* that is; these attitudes extend into our entire experience of *life*. Logic really is more important than our humanity if we need people to build weapons to defend the nation, and it's often more important than other human attributes in order to secure a job. But those priorities are almost exactly backwards for experiencing meaning in life. The only reason to sustain life by designing better weapon systems, or by making money to buy food, is if it's worth living to begin with, and better math scores will never make that happen.

---

[8] Science started in ancient Greece, and we inherited a lot from them, but *they* still realized the value of the internal. If Plato can be taken as representative of the culture, that's apparent. In *The Republic*, where he described what a perfect society would be, the education of the populace included ethics and music as major elements and not optional extraneous hobbies like we make them.

We can't see our own attitudes

Be it resolved then, again, that these attitudes are in us. But we still probably wouldn't be able to sense that. And there's a simple reason that we would miss it—we can't observe ourselves from a third-person perspective.

Members of a particular culture typically do not think about themselves so that one of them would live daily keeping in mind, "I am part of this culture so I value privacy," or "I am from this land so I am very fatalistic," or "I am hopeful" or "I have a strong sense of community because I am from this place." We are able to visit other places and spot characteristics and messages *there*. For example, it's clear that the Japanese value privacy and keeping to themselves.[9] Anyone could pick up on that during just a short stay there. And the Greeks value leaving sleeping dogs to lie where they are. But we can't visit ourselves to see how *we* think. We see things here and in ourselves that are all we've ever known and we say, "of course," or we don't see those things in the first place. I've read that the overwhelming impression of some people who visit America is that we are hopeful, for example, but most of us living here would have no idea of that. People incorporate the values and messages of their culture without knowing it, and without being able to recognize it usually.

It is hard for us to recognize characteristics of our own thinking, but it's still possible for us to see the effects of rationalism by observing one of our subcultures—the scientific community. Science has been the source for a lot of our worldview and, again, it was part of the driving force for the Enlightenment. Taking a look at the way it operates may be the best way to see the effect our

---

[9] Which I picked up on after three days of a trip on which myself and another big sasquatch-looking white guy walking in a sea of Japanese did not attract so much as one glance.

Enlightenment mindset has on us, since we can't look directly in the mirror to observe it.

I'll mention, for my credibility to speak here, that I have degrees in physics and electrical engineering, and I can testify that the effects of the scientific mindset are not trivial. After some amount of time working in science, the idea gets into you a little bit that life doesn't matter, and that it's inconsequential. I can remember noticing a strange kind of feeling, or lack of feeling, during the height of my studying, whenever I read or thought about anything that wasn't an area to be computed. In a lot of purely human kinds of areas, my mind would shut down in a way, and I couldn't make myself care or think as though it mattered. Research and logical truth are what are important in the physical world; the rest of it is nonsensical.

The mathematician Kurt Gödel could be taken as a good example of what this mindset does at its extreme. Although Gödel was in a situation where, if ever, a person might notice a current of change in life—1938 Austria—Amir Aczel describes that he "was oblivious to his surroundings" and that "his work in the foundations of mathematics was absorbing him, and, slowly, he was losing contact with reality." [10] He relates that when Gödel arrived at Princeton after fleeing Europe, he

> expressed surprise that there were so many refugees trying to flee Europe. Even after the difficulties he and his wife had experienced in wartime Europe, he was living in a strange internal world. When asked what life was like in Vienna before they left, Gödel replied: "The coffee was wretched."[11]

---

[10] Amir Aczel, *The Mystery of the Aleph: Mathematics, the Kabbalah, and the Search for Infinity* (New York: Pocket Books, 2000), 199.

[11] Aczel, 205.

Gödel was not born detached or oblivious, but working in the purely logical world and losing appreciation for the value and reality of other realms of life made him that way. The exclusion of anything but reason made him half-dead—still far from the condition of Tolstoy's Prince Andrei, but approaching that point.

Another indicator of what the field is like and what it requires of people, is the fact that there are almost no females in physics or electrical engineering. Those two fields are the coldest of all. The spectrum grows warmer in mechanical engineering, aerospace, civil engineering, and warmer yet in biology, and the percentage of women in those fields goes up correspondingly. That's not a coincidence. Feelings don't help to get the job done in areas that are heavy on logic, so emotions have no place there and they need to be left at the door. The male gender seems to be more comfortable with doing that.

In science, if there is no physical or logical evidence for something, it does not exist. This means that feelings don't exist and spiritual things don't exist, or, if they do, they're unimportant at best. That's the way it goes, and in science this attitude works, and it's necessary. But if anyone tried extending that kind of thinking to life overall, they would have a big pr...well, *we've already done that*! This is what rationalism is about—stretching logic to cover *all things* and seeing all things only through that filter, discounting everything else.

Doing this will affect us deeply. It's possible that devoting most of our thought and energy to a particular approach or viewpoint actually even causes a physical change in our brains. One article on that topic quotes Charles Darwin from an autobiography he'd written near the end of his life:

> I have said that in one respect my mind has changed during the last twenty or thirty years. Up to the age of thirty, or beyond it, poetry of many kinds...gave me great pleasure, and even as a schoolboy I took intense delight in

> Shakespeare....I have also said that formerly pictures gave me considerable, and music, very great delight. But now for many years I cannot endure to read a line of poetry: I have tried to read Shakespeare, and found it so intolerably dull that it nauseated me. I have also almost lost any taste for pictures or music. ...I retain some taste for fine scenery, but it does not cause me the exquisite delight which it formerly did. ... My mind seems to have become a kind of machine for grinding general laws out of large collections of facts, but why this should have caused the atrophy of that part of the brain alone, on which the higher tastes depend, I cannot conceive...The loss of these tastes is a loss of happiness, and may possibly be injurious to the intellect, and more probably to the moral character, by enfeebling the emotional part of our nature.[12]

The author of the article argues that a focus on logical exercises at the neglect of artistic or emotional thoughts physically shifts the balance of an individual's brain to strength in logic and weakness in artistic or emotional capacity. That wouldn't surprise me at all because that's what it feels like. I've experienced it, and I still do experience it every day.

These examples are extreme cases. These are people who work in the area of logic and proof all their lives and who are most dedicated to those things at the exclusion of all else. But it is generally agreed that the same attitudes are in the psyche of the entire population.

It hurts us, but is it *true*

So, rationalism has affected us negatively as well as positively, but I would say that if the empirical view of the world is

---

[12] Virginia Owens, "Seeing Christianity in Red & Green as Well as Black & White," *Christianity Today*, 27, no. 13 (Sept 2, 1983): 38.

right, then it's right, and any negative effects of it on us are just too bad. I would never condone a voluntary retreat to ignorance for any reason. However, the view is simply incorrect to begin with. This is shown both in the meaninglessness of the world without feelings, and in the fact that the physical world that rationalism emphasizes as being all that exists, is really no more solid than a feeling itself.

Fellow humans should listen and consider this: Atoms, as one example, are not little golf balls held together by our familiar, comfortable idea of forces. Particles are waves of probability and forces are communicated from one wave thing to another by other particle-waves, which carry information about what the force they represent is. When atoms "collide," it is not like two pool balls connecting on a smaller scale. It's an interaction more similar to basic entities meeting and communicating to each other what they are and how fast they are traveling, then accepting or not accepting each other's information. If this seems familiar or intuitive, it shouldn't, because it definitely is not.

There really *is* no such thing as "solid" and, after looking closely enough at the physical world for a long enough time, a nagging suspicion might begin to grow that, in the end, the whole thing seems a lot like an *idea*. I resorted to that conclusion after several years, and I've run across hints and a few plain statements of the same thing from professional physicists. An immaterial disappearing virtual particle wave is just not all that real and logical whereas an idea or feeling that a person has is imaginary or inconsequential. And there isn't a single scientist in the world who could say differently, because a scientist's job is not to determine what things *mean*. Their job is only to discover how they work. Any living being who can turn his gaze upon these things and consider them has about an equal shot at understanding what they *mean*, or of appreciating them, regardless of education, and probably regardless of intelligence as well.

Again, virtual particles, immaterial energy, transfer of momentum through information exchange by carrier particles, laws that could be other than they are, but are not...*that* is the solid world that we take comfort in and think exists in and of itself? This is not realistic. It seems to me that the entire physical universe is as much an idea as any supposedly insubstantial feeling that we can ever have (although clearly not our idea), so it is not true that the physical world is substantial whereas our thoughts and feelings are insubstantial; contrary to modern thinking. If there is a God then there is spirit, but even if there isn't a God, the physical world is still almost as much of a ghost as anything else. Our attitude of treating the physical and "rational" as though it is real and important whereas the spiritual is unreal or unimportant is wrong either way.

There have been good and bad effects of our modern emphasis on reason. Not many people live in fear of tree spirits or sacrifice their kids to fire gods now, and application of the standard issue MK-1-BRAIN has brought a lot of freedom from stupidity and superstition in general. Those good effects of the Enlightenment and rationalism have been commonly recognized. But the harmful ones haven't been.

It should be clear from the discussion above, or just from a couple minutes of reflection, that life without feeling is meaningless, and that feeling or emotion is the real essence of life. So, a little logic could be applied to tell us that impressing on people that what they feel isn't real, or that it doesn't matter, would kill a part of their ability to live. Cultural impact is hard to see when we can't know anything other than our generation's situation and mindset, but we were born in this age and it would be naïve to think the message of the times has not affected us all. Before the age of logic the western mindset and message was that the heart and the spiritual was more real and more important than anything else. That mindset was right, but it is not ours.

The Decision

My story didn't end with that summer in 1996, although a few times I've wished that it had. Life changed overnight for me after the events of July 4th. There was really no way it couldn't have after a day like the one that happened to me, and after the way it had been led up to. I remember the overwhelming comfort I had afterwards because I knew there was a God and that he would not let existence be meaningless. I'd entered what felt like a permanent shelter, whereas it had been like floating in cold, dark space before. And the weight of things I wished weren't true, but that I was resigned to, was no longer on my own shoulders. That day I stopped smoking weed and drinking. And for a long time I didn't go around the people I had spent my time with before. There was no way that I could take the new thing that was in me back into the same situation, so I left my friends and my old life completely.

Every morning when I woke up after July 4th, the first thing I did was to get the Bible my brother had—since I didn't have one—and read it in my bed. I read it all day alternately with sleeping and just lying there basking in the new peace I had, until I went to sleep at night. I can't even remember leaving my room during those weeks except for a couple times. After a few days of this I gave up putting the Bible back on my brother's desk when I went to sleep, and tucked it next to the mattress in the top bunk of the bunk-bed I slept on. When I woke up the next morning I would take it out and start reading without even getting out of bed, and when I went to sleep I would tuck it back there.

That went on for about six weeks and it was the best time of my life. A better description actually would be that it was like an entirely different life, in a place and condition I've never known before or since. I was certain that God had prepared a place for me in heaven and that, indeed, all this stuff was true after all; no fairy tale and no wishful thinking. That was absolutely incredible to me. I could also sense that he was always with me, every day and every second, and I was able to appreciate those things in the same way that I had appreciated what a universe without God would have meant before.

So, I wish that the things worth writing in a book had ended there, or that they'd gone on in some kind of way close to what they should have. But that wasn't what happened. That new experience didn't gradually fade away or get old as I got used to it, like the novelty wearing off a new toy or situation. What caused it to end, instead, was me making the worst decision I've ever made. I'm sorry to have to tell what I do in the next couple chapters, but it is what happened.

I had enjoyed hanging out smoking weed and drinking before July 4, 1996. That part of the old life had been fun, especially in the summer, but there was no more of it for me. As I was thinking about that one day, I decided, rather lightly, that I would give up my new life, go back and do those things again for a while, research everything over again so that I would be more sure and wouldn't have to struggle as much to retain my faith, and then I would come back.

I was sitting in the back of a car while those thoughts went through my mind over about two minutes, and as we were about to get to the route 123 overpass over the interstate, I made my decision. I remember it perfectly. As soon as I decided this, it hit me how serious what I had just done was, and the sound of a huge bell being struck that second would have been a fitting sound to accompany the feeling I got. And that feeling turned out not to be misplaced either, because nothing has ever been the same in the seventeen years that have passed since that moment.

I hadn't forgotten what I'd seen, but I ignored it and went back to the same old things I was doing before, with the same people; although I wasn't feeling so good inside while I did it. I became confused again right away, my peace vanished, and I was hurting again. It only took about a month of that before I made another about-face and tried to return to the new life I'd decided to take a break from. I stopped drinking and smoking again, and I went to church for the first time since my last attendance at age six. But I have never gotten back to the place I was at after I first believed.

At first, after July 4th, I could feel that things were different, and something had obviously changed. I had felt then like a human being *should* feel, and the way that all human beings wish they could feel. My anxiety, for example, which I had always battled and almost always lost to, was completely gone. *Poof.* That had never, ever happened before. I also didn't have to go out anywhere, do anything, or wrestle with myself in order to be at peace. I was perfectly happy just sitting in silence with myself and God. And the peace that I had went deep. I remember a couple times thinking about the rest of the world and feeling sorry for them because of the life they live here; because I knew they didn't have it. Ever since my decision to go back to what I was doing before, though, things have never been right again, aside from a few brief moments interspersed over many years.

Largely, or mostly, because of the fact of things never being okay again, most of the story of my Christian life has centered on the single issue of whether I really *am* a Christian. That concern began soon after I made my decision in the back of the car that summer, and I asked myself that question constantly for 20 years afterwards. And it has been very far from just an academic issue to me. Fear of the possibility that I was going to hell crushed everything inside of me for six years of my youth—from seventeen until I was twenty-two and started to get over it a little bit, or, at least, to be distracted enough not to despair completely. So the extreme nature of my experience continued. I don't have to make this stuff up.

I want to say again that I'm sorry that the story of my life has to take a steep downward turn here. Turning back from the creator of this whole universe was the biggest mistake I've ever made, and it was also probably the worst thing I have ever done. If there was anything I could change that I have ever done in my life, it would have been this; no question about it. There isn't even a close second. However, either way, for good or bad, if I had kept going forward and had not made that decision, I might have had nothing else to say. My story would have stopped earlier with something like, "And he walked with God all his days, then was buried with his fathers." As it is, though, I have a lot more to say about my experience that is very much worth putting on paper, and some of it might help someone else. And the help might come primarily in a warning that I can go on and put in one sentence right here: If you find yourself with faith in Jesus Christ, and at peace doing what you should be doing, do not *ever* throw it away. You might never regain what you will lose.

Before getting into the rest of the story I will say something very important to help put the issue of salvation into context. For centuries most adherents of the Christian religion—which, of course, was everyone in Europe in the past—hoped that they wouldn't be going to hell and hoped that they just might go to heaven...as if life didn't have pains enough already without fear of eternal punishment added on. But the main reason for that doubt and confusion was that the clergy, who were presumably teachers, were as blind as the blindest people that could be found if recruiters were sent out to discover them, and they had apparently never actually read the Bible. What I learned in about five minutes of study as a teenager, they seem to have never grasped. If what the Bible says is true, forgiveness of sins and promise of heaven is a gift given through faith; not by attending church, eating magic bread, baptism, saying prayers regularly, or being good. And it is a guarantee, not a hope or a maybe.[13] There is no need for someone who believes in Jesus Christ to wonder about his fate, and all of the Christians I've known, with just a couple of exceptions, are confident of heaven.

But for several reasons, and good ones really, I did wonder about my own fate and I just could not get passed it. Anyone can believe anything, or see strange visions from being delusional or from huffing spray paint and junk, but a person being transformed demonstrates something else that is genuine and powerful. That transformation happened to me, but after two months I abandoned everything I could have ever hoped to gain because I missed getting messed up and hanging out. And things were never the same after that decision, despite my very best efforts to make them the same. This is the reason I wondered about my condition.

I didn't know why there was no power in any of it for me anymore, why it no longer worked, or why I felt as badly as I ever had before. It was worse than before, actually. I suspected the problem was my faith—that I had never been able to recover the simple confidence of the truth of the things in the Bible again. But I wasn't sure of that, and I didn't know what it meant if it was true. I also didn't know how to answer verses like this one, for example: "Jesus replied, 'No one who puts his hand to the plow and looks back is fit for service in the kingdom of God'" (Luke 9:62). That seemed to describe me exactly.

---

[13] One of the many statements of that teaching is this: "Everyone who looks to the Son and believes in him shall have eternal life, and I will raise him up at the last day" (John 6:40). Or when a guard at a jail Paul was in asked what he had to do to be saved, Paul said, "Believe in the Lord Jesus, and you will be saved" (Acts 16:31). "Saved" meaning, forgiven, guaranteed heaven. There are somewhere around fifty other passages saying this same thing and there are no qualifiers in any of them.

Several other passages didn't help much either, but I was also able to come to a simple conclusion on my own, very easily, without having to *read* anything. Just looking at my previous state, looking at what I'd done in abandoning it, and then observing my current state, seemed to say it all. I had tried to get back to where I had been—with a peace, and a conscious connection to God, and a faith that I knew I had—or at least to some place where things were okay, but I could never come anywhere close. If all was forgiven, why was that the case? The most obvious conclusion was that I had lost my salvation when I abandoned Christ, and that God had abandoned me forever. I was *damned*. I remember very well the first time that thought ever occurred to me, the first month of the next school year, and, as I said, it never left.

I had some of the normal problems and weaknesses then that a kid will have, in addition to that very unusual one, but, again, I certainly was not a kid. Kids are sheltered by their parents, they are goofs, and they have barely ever extended a toe beyond what everyone around them believes. They also have a built in assumption they can be protected and that the world is okay. That wasn't me. The previous year I had done my very best to leave any comfort, and to know what was true, and not to delude myself if there really was no hope. I had believed previously that there was not a God, and I had faced what that meant. Now it seemed most likely that I was going to hell, and I was in position to face all of what *that* would mean also; making perfect conditions for my suffering.

Not a second of a single day passed by during that year, or several years following, that everything I saw and felt wasn't colored by an abiding terror. I still tried very hard to do everything I should and to keep living like some kind of prophet or something. I was always reading the Bible and spending time at church; I never cussed, didn't drink or smoke, didn't look at girls, behaved differently around other people, etc., etc., etc. But it was horrible.

The Decision   41

During that last year of high school, every morning when I woke up, the first thought in my mind was to wonder if I was really saved, and the second was to think that I probably wasn't. No, I was probably going to hell.

I did everything I could think of to fix the problem and to make things right again—to force myself to change, to accept, to relinquish, or to do whatever it was that I must have needed to do to get things right. And I will repeat that my best guess at the problem was that I no longer believed any of it like I had at first. I simply wasn't able to. The faith that I'd first had made everything work. And I could feel it. I no longer had that faith afterwards, but I did try to get it back.

Once, at the end of my last year of high school, for example, over five days, I ate one muffin, and only allowed myself that so I wouldn't pass out—trying to force whatever was wrong to become right, and maybe to force God to do something.[14] It didn't work. In fact, I had nightmares of hell a couple of those nights.

In comparison to those new times, life had been just a big picnic of fun in previous years.[15]

Ah, youth. Those golden days.

Even in talking or writing about it now, at age thirty-four, after years of perspective gained, study, and some other memorable

---

[14] And this five days without food was much more serious than it would be for most people since I barely ate anything in the first place and didn't have one ounce of fat to burn.

[15] I'll interject the thought into the narrative at this point that experiencing these things might seem crazy to some people, but I hit very high marks on sanity. A lot of religious things that people have done over the ages have been very stupid, but they're usually not actually insane. And mine wasn't even stupid. Something that *is* insane, though, that I can also mention, is for people to go through life not knowing and not caring in the least to find out answers, with death coming closer all the time. That is what almost everybody in this world does, and *that* is insanity. Concern for eternity is logical.

events happening that showed that God is still with me, it is still a little scary. It's difficult to describe how bad it is to believe you're damned, or what it does to a person, especially after what I had experienced before. This letter that I'd written to a friend when I was twenty-five expresses it about as well as I can:

> The only thing that matters to me is salvation—whether I am saved. Certain things indicate to me that I must be, but other things indicate that I am not, or that I have lost my salvation. What I go by is the hope that I am. There is no bottom to the terror of hell. Who knows how much destruction the condemnation that I'm going to burn forever has wreaked inside me over the years. Certainly it is a -------. It will make you hate God if you think he's sending you to hell. I can't think of anything worse in anyone's life than having this fear. There is nothing worse. Hell is the worst thing in this existence and I have wished that the creation, or at least myself, was never made because of it.

Now I have some defense but, then, as a young man, I had no perspective and no defense at all. Even now also, after all my learning, it still appears in a lot of ways that I did hand back the new life God had given me, saying, "I don't want this," and that he accepted it back and allowed me to change course to the flames. I had no argument against that conclusion for years of my youth. On the contrary, I had a tendency—as I still do—to believe and to embrace the worst.

      And I never told anyone about any of this. I couldn't go to a school guidance counselor or some other poor ignoramus, even if I would have been willing to. They knew nothing. And I couldn't go to my parents, even if I would have, because they also knew nothing. I wasn't going to have smoke blown at me before I found out that there was a God, and I wasn't going to start looking for a hole to hide in afterwards either. So there was no comfort for me. If the problem was what I thought it was, no one could change it and no one could help me anyway. So I stared at it right in the face all the time, and all I could do was to keep breathing and trying to get things right, hoping that what I thought to be most likely, was not true.

All of this is not the best presentation for the Christian faith and I'll mention that I've hesitated to share it here. But I do not like it when things are sugar-coated, and I just will not do that myself. I prefer getting all of the truth, even if reality is unpleasant or even crushing. Also, this is what *happened*, and if I cut it out, it wouldn't tell the story. I think that very little that occurs in this world has anything to do with God's will, but that some things *are* his doing for some purpose, and, again, all of this that I've experienced may have had some reason after all—maybe just to be told for the benefit of someone else. So I am going to make sure that I tell all of it and not just the nice parts.[16]

For that reason, to tell the whole story, I should also mention another aspect of what was going on then. Over those years of misery I still used to try to make myself internalize better that life was a breath, and to try to test myself by considering how I would respond in some extreme situation. Just like before, the goal was to prepare for things that might happen so that I could do everything and anything that I might have to for honor and right; as if I was getting ready for war. I would think about the theoretical scenarios—that I will simply say, really were not pleasant ideas, always involving the most crucible-like events of my death or horrible injury—very seriously, determined that I must never fail.

---

[16] I will also repeat that Jesus came to save the world, not to condemn it. And for those that believe what he said, there is no need to doubt what's going to happen after death (other than the human handicap for believing anything we can't see or prove). Again, in about fifty places the same thing is said, "Everyone who looks to the Son and believes in him shall have eternal life, and I will raise him up the last day" (John 6:40). It does not say, "*might* have eternal life" or "I will raise him up *unless he...*"

I'll also interject here to say that I now know the answer to all those questions and self-testing that I used to do. The answer is that I couldn't, wouldn't, and can't handle it. I'm not any kind of ideal being and, despite all my preparation and oaths on my soul to always do right, and to never betray, I would probably become a panicked, unfaithful animal like anyone else if the wrong thing happened. I finally learned and admitted that if the communists in some country I was working in hung me by my nose and put my privates in a vise, I don't have much doubt that I would say anything they wanted me to about anyone or anything. "Jesus? No, don't know him, don't believe it. Never believed it. America? Never liked it. It's evil. Excuse me? Yes, you're right, I am a fairy cupcake. Sing it? *Ohhh, I'm a fairy cupcake short and sweet...*" I have no doubt of that now. The only person who doesn't have limits and would never fail is God himself. Every other single person in the world will chicken out, give out the codes to blow up his country or whatever, betray his friends and family, deny all his beliefs, and otherwise crack completely; it will just be a matter of degree. Everyone can be very sure of that.

I realize my shortcomings and limits now, and I learned it by the time I got to be about twenty-three so that I could understand a little better. But in those first horrible years, I didn't, and I was not laughing one little bit about any of this. And I just made things that much worse by my self-training program.

The fun all ended

Indeed, that time was horrible, and no comparison to the experiences of anyone else in this world could make that fact untrue. But I've come to the point now where I should describe the *worst* time of my life, when all of the relative fun I'd been having before came to an end. It was always very bad after I'd made the decision to go back to what I'd been doing before my salvation, but four weeks during my first year of college, at age nineteen, were the most painful thing I've ever experienced. The cause was the same, but with the horror intensified.

The thing that started this new event happened one day during an art history class that I had to take for my degree. The teacher showed a painting of Christ on the cross and she was describing the history and background of it, when a terrible thought went through my mind that seemed to me then to be an acceptance of the truth at last: "*I don't know him!*" meaning, "I'm not saved and after I die I'm going to hear, 'Depart from me into everlasting torment. I never knew you.'"

The bottom really dropped out then. Every day before that, I had wondered and asked myself if I was really a Christian. Throughout that time I had thought that I probably really knew the answer but that I wasn't willing to admit it. That day in the classroom, though, I thought that I had finally accepted the answer that I'd known the whole time but wouldn't accept:

"*I am damned!*"

I walked back to my dorm room when the class ended and I can remember sitting on my bed, feeling my heart actually physically struggling inside my chest from the stress, and noting to myself in a detached way that my heart might actually give out. But that was the least of my problems. For about a month after that, I was in a world of terror every waking moment. And I never really slept. Every night was a strange type of half-waking nightmare.

Years before, I had known that no one could change things or give any comfort for reality, so when the stuff had happened the previous year, I had just taken it and had known that there was nowhere to run to. During those weeks after the bottom dropped out, though, I finally told someone else for the first time that all was not well inside me—not that it shouldn't have already been obvious enough for anyone to notice if they'd had the faculty of either sight or hearing.

I talked to friends, and also even called my parents to talk, which really indicated the kind of condition I was in. I had never one time since having grown up, expressed any personal concern or trouble to them and, of course, had never asked anyone in my family about any spiritual issue. I was still very well aware after the class that day that they knew nothing, but I called them because I knew they loved me. Maybe they could help protect me from God a little bit.

Throughout those weeks, I also discovered something else that horrified me, when I observed a couple of my feelings. On one of those grand old collegiate days I found a place I could be alone in a study room in one of the dorms, and I sat down, and I looked into my heart, and I found that I hated Jesus Christ and saw him as my enemy. Naturally, that terrified me even more, because I figured that it further sealed and settled what my fate was.

I almost dropped out of school and left. I went for three days with no food at one point, determined to make myself believe in Christ. And for me, being a person who already had no fat to burn and never ate much, this incident—along with the previous one during my last year of high school—of going without food was extreme. For the sake of forever, though, what measure would be too drastic to bring about a solution?

And the rationale behind this attempt to make myself believe was that I knew the verses that guarantee forgiveness and eternal life. Those things are free gifts, given to anyone who believes. Faith is the only requirement, but it was something that I was pretty sure I didn't have. I had known what it felt like to believe it all when I had first entered that new life after July 4th, and it definitely wasn't like that anymore. I didn't have anything that worked. What I had was dread, anxiety, terror, and pain.

I can illustrate that part of my condition a little bit in one conversation I had with the leader of a campus ministry I went to then. I told him that I wasn't sure I was saved. He asked if I believed in Jesus Christ, and I had to say, "I don't know." That is a strange place to be. To have to say, "yes, of course I believe it. But I don't know that I do really."

I tried to make something give, and to get some kind of breakthrough. I gave it quite an effort, part of which included my starvation attempt. But it didn't work either, except to make life even worse, which turned out to, in fact, still be possible.

Oh yes, to be a kid again.

The fun resumed, back to normal

I was finally pulled out of this hole, back to the situation of things being only as bad as they had been in the previous two years, by an experience that was probably God's doing. I figured that if I was damned, he wouldn't do anything for me at all. So, after I was pulled out of it, I went on about as I had before—still trying, and still hurting, *badly*. It was all inside, though. No one seemed to notice and no one ever asked. I was pretty well accustomed to functioning normally, to all appearances, despite being flayed inside. I would even joke a fair amount through all the years and could appear to be pretty much alright, except for that one month. Things were still far from okay after that period ended, but they were never as bad again as they had been in the first couple years.

When I look at that worst time in hindsight with the experience I have now, I'm struck for one thing that I could get through it without having some kind of major, long lasting emotional trauma or stress disorder—things that would keep me from being able to even function in the world. I also notice that there was not one tear through all of it; not in that month and not in the two horrible years before. Not a single tear or whimper.[17] Two years after that worst month, though, I do remember walking into someone's office, of all places, and tears starting out of nowhere, for no reason, and not being able to hold it back. After all I'd gone through, though, I couldn't blame myself if I had to be cared for by my mother for the rest of my life and fed soup through a straw.

However, that time ended, and I didn't die, and I have some wisdom I can share from dealing with all of this for years: Firstly, it would be no wonder if I had hated God. I still had a human heart and real emotions, as it turned out. And constantly thinking that he was going to send me to hell...no one is going to love him after that or come through it without resentments. That is simply the way it is, and I can understand very well if somebody has a personal problem with God, or an animosity. Not that it's right, but *I know;* better than most anyone, including whoever that person might be. Also, the thoughts and emotions I saw in myself then were immensely disturbing to me, but I learned that nothing that I can think or feel can shock God like it might shock the archetypical characterization of the cloistered priest that we picture him to be. He's a lot bigger than any of us typically appreciate. I learned that. And, my realization while looking at the painting of Christ on the cross, "*I don't know him!*" is no wonder either. I don't even really know him now it seems like to me a lot of the time, and I'm acquainted with very, very few people who show evidence of really knowing him. There are degrees in a lot of things that I used to think were simply on or off.

Also, if the Bible is true, the only way to establish a relationship with God is through Jesus Christ, so, whoever accepts him has that. But something I've also figured out over the years is that very few Christians have ever known God as closely as I was

---

[17] ...And yet I wonder now why I usually feel nothing, or why I'm tired a lot.

able to know him for a brief time that summer. For a long time I thought that every other person who believed must have experienced a connection to the Creator like the one I had during those first months. But that was very naïve and far from the truth. It seems obvious that circumstances, decisions, and possibly providence, do not ever bring many people to a place like that in this world. I know they have never brought me there again.

Lastly, I also learned many years later, that if there is such a thing as salvation, it cannot be lost.

Today, and for some years past, I smile a lot and I am well. I can also say that I like all kinds of people, and that all kinds of people seem to enjoy my company: hedonists, atheists, guys who just got out of jail or are in jail, bookworms, misfits, drug addicts, and straight arrows. But it is hard to describe how horrifying and painful things were for a long time—years and years, of my youth. They were the very worst days and, as for other things, it could just never be communicated. Things got better only over many years.

Anger

By this point I wish again that I could talk about something happy, but that's still not possible yet if I'm going to tell the story truly. I got most of the way out of the pit of despair I had been in that first year of college, but I still had the same doubts, and whatever had been wrong before was still wrong after. Through the following years I kept breathing and walking; living with it. About seven years passed before the next thing worth mentioning happened.

To repeat: forever after the time I decided to abandon the new faith I'd gained, still at age seventeen, things were as described. This may be a little repetitive also, but I'll emphasize again that in those first years, and through the next seven that I'll skip over, I still tried my best to be and to do everything that I should, in order to be a good ambassador of Jesus Christ, and to somehow fix what was wrong with me. Over many periods I was disciplined and dedicated, refraining from this and that, praying and studying, and even telling a few people what the Bible said about eternal life. But all the while I was hurting, badly, and experiencing the same absolute dryness and unreality of it all, always believing that I was probably going to hell. The Bible promises that God's gift of eternal life is available, not that happiness in this life if going to be yours too. But it still would have been pretty hard to miss the irony of how my life was while I was trying to be an example to others: *"And if you believe in Christ, you too can have what I have!"* The irony wasn't lost on me.

Those were the simple facts. But those facts never made me angry until after quite a few years of suffering, when I was twenty-five. Until that time, I wouldn't allow or admit anything like a resentment towards God for what had happened. I was too loyal. But I remember driving down to move stuff out of school one day in the summer, and for the first time objectively considering for the first time the conditions and circumstances of how something could devastate a young person like this thing had devastated and abused me. I took a look at it from a removed perspective, and it finally made me angry.

If any counselor or impartial observer had glanced at my situation he could have easily concluded something like this:

> The subject acquired religious belief as teenager and, aside from an initial period of several months, the new religion has caused intense emotional pain. He has experienced no relief from this at any time past, nor is any relief anticipated in the future. Effects may include deep scarring and hindered development; may have permanently decreased subject's energy and desire to live.

Those observations would be exactly accurate, and starting on that day when I was twenty-five, after about a third of my life spent in that unique misery, I could finally see it in a way that would allow real feelings. And I became very angry and didn't let it go for a long time.

The cause of my reaction, and the depth of it, deserves as much explanation as I can give it. I've only ever found one other place that the kind of thing I suffered from has been described. Lucretius (ca. 99 BC – ca. 55 BC) said,

> if people saw that there is a fixed limit to oppressive cares, with some reason they would be strong enough to fight back against religious beliefs and the threats of seers. As it is,

there is no means of resisting, no power, since death must bring with it the fear of eternal punishment.[18]

I can say that people can be tough enough to deal with some very difficult things—anything the world can dump on them. They can overcome crippling fears and weaknesses inside themselves, and injustice or frightening situations outside themselves. But *no one* can handle fear of punishment after death; of being thrown into a pit: "...there is no means of resisting, no power..." The idyllic triumphant and noble spirit that has overcome and that has been strengthened and that is sailing along bravely through the perils and fears of life like a figurehead...that spirit will be crushed without ceremony if a fear of damnation is encountered; whereas that person might have overcome everything else before, and might have continued to overcome everything else in the future otherwise. Whatever I personally was or was not, it certainly crushed me and I probably never have recovered, and never will. It will always be a part of me.

Lucretius also said, "the fear of Acheron must be thrown violently out the door. This fear throws human life into deep and utter confusion, staining everything with the black darkness of death, and leaves no pleasure clear and pure."[19] That is also a fact. I said before that it colored everything I saw or thought, every second. This is what Lucretius meant. When I went to the amusement park it was with me, when I watched a movie it was with me, when I went to a tournament at Virginia Beach, it was with me and it was always dominating my thoughts and emotions. For the one at the beach, for example, years later I saw a picture that my mother had taken of me there, and little did she or anyone else know. But I know. When I

---

[18] Lucretius, (Titus Lucretis Carus) *On the Nature of Things* (book 1, vs. 107-11) Ancient, 324

[19] Ibid., (book 3, vs. 37-40). Ancient philosophy, 335

looked at that picture later, what I saw was the pain that was always eating me inside, and the specter of horror that lived right in the middle of my life. And I saw that I had no help.

And it wouldn't matter where I was: for any picture I might look at from that time, that's what I would see, because that's what was going on, without a second's escape. *Nothing* is left unaffected by the looming dread, and there was never a time that I forgot entirely. I saw and felt life and everything in it through *fire* colored glasses that never came off.

That was the main aspect of my pain over those years, of course, and it was the main reason for my eventual anger, but I should also mention another thing from those earlier years that was more fuel for the fire of resentment after it started, although it was minor in comparison to the first. I think it's worth diverging to describe it.

The other fuel source

Before I had believed in Jesus Christ, another fact I had finally learned during that previous year was an important lesson about the behavior that's required of males in order for them to be able to live with themselves or to have the freedom of self-respect. This thing is a big deal to any young man especially, because the world is different as a kid. Adults usually leave each other alone and they're courteous, but young people are not. Public schools and the surrounding society are a viper pit for anyone except those few strange or lucky people who seem to be oblivious to it, and to float right through.

To put it briefly, I was well aware in my life before the events of July 4th changed things for me, that some particular people out there that I knew and did not like, very possibly might say something to me, unprovoked, as had happened plenty of times before. I had resolved about a year before I'd experienced faith, that

I would never be trampled on again. And what that means is violence. That *is* the only solution in a lot of situations.[20] In truth, by that last year before the summer of 1996, I would have rather bled to death than let anything go without a reply. I'd finally learned that it wasn't as if I had a choice about it. Knowing the moral resolutions I had made within myself that no one else could see, and knowing that I didn't do it for the opinion of anyone else on this earth, and as quiet as I kept it all to myself...after all that, the possibility of being spit upon had become something that I could not let happen to me. I owed it to myself.

I'd finally learned by that time that certain things *had* to be done—whether there was fear or anger, or whether there was neither. Some people learn this lesson faster, and it's easier for them because they're simply stronger, but it took me a while and it was not easy at all. Despite having the weak and fearful vessel of myself to live and work with, though, I had gotten there, and I had gained a taste of freedom and self-respect with that arrival, at long last. This whole issue might sound petty to some people, but that would only be because they have no idea and have never experienced it. Those who know, know exactly what I'm talking about, and that it matters.

One example that demonstrates the point was in a class that third year of high school before the summer of 1996. I was minding my own business, as always, and there was some debate between two tables about the number of books at one or the other table, when somebody that I had never once spoken to called me something. At that moment was the only time in my life that my vision has actually been affected by anger. I started yelling at him and the whole class went silent. The other kid was scared to death and didn't make a sound. And I was spoken to differently by people in that class afterwards. But I didn't take any sense of victory in that. It was pure anger.

---

[20] Although that violence is for God to carry out rather than for us most of the time.

However, a few minutes afterwards, *I was okay*. And that's the important part, and the reason for mentioning it. A few years earlier if anything like it had happened I wouldn't have been anywhere close to okay. And, further, going day to day just a few years before I was *never* anywhere close to okay, whether anything happened or not, because I had no self-respect and didn't know what I needed to do, and I hadn't possessed anything in myself worth protecting anyway. Later, though, I *was* alright. After a lot of difficulty to learn the lesson, and years of pain, I had learned it, and I could feel the freedom that came with it.

So, that's just how things work(ed), and how they had to be, and I was as ready as I could make the frail vessel of myself to be for pistols at noon by the old oak tree, pipes in the parking lot, or for whatever else it might have to be. I can say that there is a feeling that comes with making those decisions—a determination to act on principle, rather than caving in and being part of the *pecking order*, and of being another participant in the ugliness and shame and cowardice. As I described earlier, for months I had thought about all these things, and I had sworn. And that time did have some effect. I'd finally been able to climb out of the muck far enough to reach a little bit of freedom and, weak as I still was, I had gone from being a spineless nothing, to actually being something. The pain I had known years before—the pain that, again, is one like no other—of being trampled on, and of knowing that I was nothing; it was gone. *Victory!* I had gotten there. I was someone serious, and upright, and nobody could tread on me. I could feel this, and I wouldn't have traded it for anything. Other than my salvation, it was probably the most precious thing I've ever had.

However, I lost those things, and I lost that feeling after I became a Christian. After becoming a Christian I wasn't allowed to live knowing that I was someone who had earned respect and that could not be spit on, and I had to take whatever anybody might say or do. I was no longer allowed to do anything about it. And if one of those incidents had happened *after* my new faith, I would have had to just sit there. And it would have torn me up inside. And, sure enough, plenty of those incidents *did* happen afterwards, and they did tear me up inside. People that I would have honestly wrecked before, could now treat me with no respect at all. Once again I was neutered, toothless, nothing; and all the feeling that went with that was back.

One particular event stands out to me that demonstrates the difference, and the effect of this loss. It involved the exact kind of persons I liked least. And, to come straight out with it, this kind were the kids who liked to pretend they grew up in a ghetto and chose to trample other people as long as it looked like it would be safe to trample them, based on their physical appearance. They are a good definition for cowardice and a good example of despicable. And just the thought of that kind of behavior used to make me truly angry and truly resolved to go all the way down with them as far as I had to go. But that was before. And this example was *after* I could no longer demand respect or do anything about it.

I was twenty years old, out somewhere, and put simply, something was said and a gesture was made, with no cause. It was the exact kind of situation in which I would have done whatever I had to do before. *Before*, I would have been alright; possibly in jail for assault or knocked out on the ground, but alright. But now that part of my identity was gone, and I wasn't allowed to do anything, it hit me like a stab wound in the heart. The pain that I'd known many years before of having some --- -- ------- *just like that* be able to push me, and of not having what it took to do something about it, and of feeling like I was nothing, was back! The feeling of self-loathing, fear, and of no freedom was back, and it went deeply into me.

I remember lying on my bed that night thinking about this and feeling it, and reflecting on where and how I had lost what I'd gained. How could it happen?! It was like a nightmare where demons of the past jump up and grab you all over again. And it had by no means started just with that one incident. That one only highlighted it. I could not have helped being acutely conscious of having lost what I'd struggled so hard to achieve, and I'll never forget that feeling. In comparison to the terror of thinking I was probably damned, this other injury was just a scratch, but that was only because of how bad the first was. And God didn't help me.[21] Not at all. All of this also made me pretty angry when my feelings finally came out.

There's still a heart

Correct standing with God is of limitless worth, and I had gained that when I became a Christian (although I thought I'd lost that too) but I also did lose a big piece of something very important to me. If I had been right spiritually, as I had been for those first couple months, I would have been okay anyway, no matter what might have happened. Or if I was stronger by nature I would have been alright. But being the mess that I was, already in the continual process of being crushed by a fear of hell, this second loss was much worse.

In summary, there were very substantial sources for the anger that began when I was twenty-five. I'd been young all those years before, and I had been on my own, and I had been devastated in probably some of the worst and deepest ways possible in an emotional or mental realm. And, to this day, I don't see that there was any help or comfort given to me. I finally allowed myself to see those facts after eight years of demolished youth, and I finally allowed myself to feel something about it.

---

[21] That is something I regard as true even now, and I won't try to toe any line by saying what I don't believe to be true—that he really did help but I didn't know it, and that maybe I only saw one set of footprints in the sand because he was carrying me or something. I do not believe that. God is just, and beyond that, he's gracious, but I do not believe he helped me in any way. All I felt was pain, destruction of what I'd fought so hard to grasp, and more pain.

The truth is that if it is really by grace that God helps anyone, then it is only by mercy that he ever spares anyone; so he could not ever be obligated to help. And it's impossible that an eternal God could be less than perfect. But there is what's logically correct according to beliefs, and then there is the human heart and the human being. And they are different things. To quote another Greek: Epictetus said,

> It is not possible then for one who thinks he is harmed to take pleasure in what he thinks is the author of the harm, any more than to take pleasure in the harm itself....That is why the farmer, and the sailor, and the merchant, and those who lose wife or children revile the gods. For men's religion is bound up with their interest.[22]

This is not an accolade for human nature, it's flaw, but it's how living creatures on earth are.

The mind may dutifully say, "Yes, I've done what's shameful and it's only by God's grace that I haven't already gotten what I deserve." But the heart absolutely will not take perceived abuse without eventually growing to hate the perceived abuser. There is no way, to use my experience as the example, that an individual is going to love someone he thinks will probably be sending him to hell. The heart is what it is, and it will take only so many orders. A person can beat his feelings into submission for a while, but I think that unless the living part of him can be killed completely, what's inside of him will feel how it feels. We can order ourselves on what we are going to *do* in life, and that ability is very valuable, but we can't order ourselves so much on how we're going to feel. The heart will be what it is deep down and it cannot be controlled by us.

---

[22] Epictetus, *Manual* section 31. Ancient, 361.

This divergence from the narrative is almost over now, but I'll mention that Martin Luther understood this aspect of human beings as well. Luther was brave, he did everything he could to follow what he thought would be God's will, and he was dedicated to the message of salvation by faith—risking his life for it. So this quote from near the end of his life is surprising:

> Though I lived as a monk without reproach, I felt that I was a sinner before God with an extremely disturbed conscience. I could not believe that he was placated by my satisfaction. I did not love, yes, I hated the righteous God who punishes sinners, and secretly, if not blasphemously, certainly murmuring greatly, I was angry with God, and said, "As if, indeed, it is not enough, that miserable sinner, eternally lost through original sin, are crushed by every kind of calamity by the law of the Decalogue, without having God add pain to pain by the gospel and also by the gospel threatening us with his righteousness and wrath!" Thus I raged with a fierce and troubled conscience.[23]

I know what this is like and I would bet that Luther was shocked and also terrified by seeing these feelings in himself. He probably thought that he must be damned for sure if that's what was in him, and I expect he did his best to repress all of it.

I would not say now that I ever hated God, because I don't think that's quite true. And I'll mention, in passing, that I would rather he exist and the whole world be as bad as it is, than for everything to be great but have no creator. However, try as I might, and, no matter how logical and loyal I might have been, there were feelings inside me that finally stopped responding to orders. They had been building up for a long time.

---

[23] Martin Luther, *Preface to the Complete Edition of Luther's Latin Writings* (Wittenberg: 1545). (page 11 in my book, *Selections From his Writings*.

So those are the reasons that, after eight years of not transgressing by having a single resentful thought towards God or anything else about what had happened to me, something finally kind of gave way inside me. The *effect* was that I was angry enough to want to destroy things: to want to not just break the first layer of the door, but to put my fist all the way through it, to pick up my desk and run it through the whole window; angry enough not to care about injuring myself, or enough to hold myself hostage with the intent of threatening my own life, to make God do something or to answer me. Nothing that I said before about having the life beaten and crushed out of me through all those years was exaggerated, and I remembered it deliberately, and I would not forget it.

During these two years that my resentment burned, I still lived very cleanly, not doing anything I shouldn't, and doing a lot of things that I should, according to the Bible. Anybody who looked at my life would have seen a very disciplined and dedicated individual. But I was angry enough at what had happened, about the way I felt, and at the world and the God who made it, that I was prepared to do something very drastic.

There comes a point where something had better happen, and the only thing that stopped me from forcing something to give was that I knew I had to treat myself decently or I wouldn't have been able to finish school. I was working on a M.S. in electrical engineering at that time and it took my best effort to get it done. If not for that, I'm not sure where I would be right now or what I might have done.

I ended up not taking any drastic physical action that could highlight the point I'd gotten to then, or that would help me describe the depth of my determination to either be finished with life as it had been, or to simply be finished with life. So, like for other things, I would only be able to describe it further by throwing in more adjectives. But, in the end, what *can* anyone do who is angry at

God and wants to force him to answer, or to otherwise force change? I wasn't a juvenile to go vandalizing things or to treat other people badly. What *can* anyone do to force God to either act, or to stand by and watch, while the situation is changed, one way or another? There was no event to highlight this part of the story, which, unfortunately, may seem to have gone nowhere. So I'll go ahead and finish it.

Calm returns

In the end my anger at God was diffused, and it was surprising what did it. I was lying in bed thinking about a scenario that could happen, and I realized the sorry way that I would behave, but that God would behave like God. I believe in respect, I certainly don't think that everyone deserves an equal share of it, and I have no problem taking my place in that order. And it was this value that made the simple thought about my behavior, compared to God's behavior, affect me so much.

I saw that despite what he was, compared to what I was, and despite the difference in what the two of us would do, where it's shown who's what and who's not, he would still allow me to even talk to him, and he was still willing to even *speak* to me. And yet I dared to point my finger at him. That fact right there mostly ended my resentment towards him for all that I had suffered over all those years of my youth.

But my feelings didn't evaporate. They swiveled around to rest on something else. Whether I harbored anger at God, or not, I knew the way life had been for a long time, and could see that it promised to continue being the same for the rest of my days. I'd had enough and, one way or another, I was going to make it change. My anger shifted away from God mostly, but the determination I had to get things right, or to have an end of it completely, did result in a plan. I came up with a course of action that would force something to give—a plan of a type that psychologists would want to put someone in a monitored care facility for. I kept it in mind for many more years, but I'll describe it later.

The rest of this book

The most interesting and important part of my life happened over one year, 1996, and that has already been told. There is a little bit more worth writing about my experience, and a conclusion of sorts to my story, but it's at the end of the book. Most of the remainder of this book is about humanity's best answers in this world, and the best sense that can be made of this life we find ourselves in. And I want to mention a little bit right here of how and why I would presume that I would be able to say anything worth hearing.

It is very clear that everyone wants to give advice, and that everyone has plenty to say on the topics of religion and philosophies for life. Whether those people have even spent so much as five minutes in sincere thought doesn't stop them. If religion is brought up, the guy in jail on a fourth count of domestic abuse will have all the answers and will talk your ear off telling you all about what you should do to live a good life. And if beliefs are brought up, the person who has never honestly asked a single question about God or cared about figuring out anything, will tell you definite answers to every question you ever wondered about. It is a world of noise with paper and words, insincerity and half-truths pouring out of every crevice. I certainly don't want to add to the gigantic pile of unnecessary noise.

The experience of having been deeply troubled is not normally something that would qualify a man for anything, or that would be listed on a resumé for any job. But if the job happens to be presenting conclusions about life that are authentic or worthy, one qualification may be exactly that—having been troubled and having struggled. And from the age of sixteen to the age of about thirty, I was continually troubled by one thing or another that I have had to reconcile or figure out or come to some kind of grips with. My mind was wind-tossed throughout my entire youth. I must know and must understand and must make sense of things.

I will also add the fact that I talk very little and I think that words spoken in groups of people who are trying to discuss a particular topic should either be necessary, or not spoken at all. I have actually refused to come back to more than one group that met weekly, that I would have otherwise enjoyed, because of people there who talked at every opportunity, regardless of merit, necessity, or meaning, and forced everyone else to listen to them. I believe that people like that are not talking because they know they had something to contribute, but because they like to talk, and they didn't mind forcing everyone else to listen to them. Sharing how I feel about this might give me away as being foul natured, but that kind of behavior irritates me quite a bit. It's a lack of self-control and it's a lack of respect for other people. And I think that most books written now are the approximate literary equivalent of this kind of behavior. 9And if I thought this one was another one like that; I would have made sure not to waste the paper and add to the noise.

At age thirty-one I left my career for four years in order to write all of this. Doing this cost me about two-hundred thousand dollars and almost prevented me from ever getting a job in engineering again. I wrote it for two reasons: to tell the story of what I experienced, and to describe the things I've figured out; so that it wouldn't all be buried with me when I'm gone.

It had bothered me for several years before starting on the writing full time that, if I had died, it would be lost. I was felt that I must be sure that I got this done. And I would write it again even if it cost me my life. This book is the most important thing I will ever do, and I am confident that the following pages are worth the time it takes to read them.

We do not Understand

I want to communicate everything that I know—such as is worth knowing—about belief, knowledge, and the human condition,. Other than my own story, that is the heart of this book.

The thing that I have had to ponder more than anything else in life has been the question of what's true, and how we can be sure of it. How can we be sure that we're right, and what is it that's involved in "believing" something to begin with? How much are we even capable of certain knowledge?

Questions like these are often viewed as being pedantic; like word games that don't do any good to ask. Is there really anyone who doesn't know what it means to believe something? There is some sense to objections like these. But it's also easy to show that we would be ignorant to just dismiss questions about belief and knowledge. Looking at these issues can show us that there are some things that we really don't know that can be helpful for gaining a better grip on our own feelings, and on insecurities about our beliefs.

It's important to communicate the simple fact that many things are deeper than they first appear. And taking a look at the nature of *understanding* and *knowledge* is a good place to start in order to do that.

In our western culture especially, we view understanding in terms of intellect. When the idea of *understanding* hits our ears, thoughts come to our minds of machines, science, taxes, and math—

things that a smart person can understand and that others can't. Our western view is that the best indicator of understanding and knowledge would be the ability to check boxes and pass scored tests. Our perceptions about knowledge are all framed in terms of logic and facts, and our common assumption is that understanding is done by the intellect alone.

And, of course, that idea is not right. The truth is that we understand things with our whole being, and it's impossible to truly know anything without our emotions and our heart being involved. A computer can have worlds of information in it, and it can perform logical operations just like the human intellect, but it cannot, and does not, *know* anything. A computer is even further away from being able to understand anything. And if this is true, and the simple possession of facts does not constitute knowledge, it means that emotions are not the only elements that are exclusive to living entities; but that "knowledge" is also found in living beings, and nowhere else in this universe. Only a subjective, feeling life can doubt, know, understand, or be certain. Clearly, questions about these things are not worthless games.

Like Forrest Gump, I don't remember being born, but I do remember, when I must have been four or five years old, that I understood that I did not used to be here, but that now I would exist forever. I can remember lying on my bed thinking about that, as just a small child new to life, and I don't think that I've ever since understood it in such a profound way again as I did then.

Tolstoy expressed a similar idea in his most well-known book:

> Prince Andrei's little son was seven years old. He could barely read, he knew nothing. He lived through many things after that day, acquiring knowledge, power of observation, experience; but if he had then possessed all these abilities he acquired later, he would not have been able

to understand the full meaning of the scene he saw take place between his father, Princess Marya, and Natasha any better, any more profoundly, than he understood it now.[24]

This thing that we call *understanding* is composed of more than just factual knowledge, and the degree to which we have it is not determined by how much information we've accumulated, or by how intelligent we are. Just those couple thoughts and examples above would be all I would personally need to make a conclusion about the topic, but a couple more things can still be added that are worthwhile.

Again, there's more to understanding than simple possession of facts, but the degree to which we have—or, more accurately, do *not* have—understanding, is not admitted, or is not evident to most people. This was clear in a story that a mathematician friend from Wyoming told me. He's probably one of the very smartest people I've met, but he said that he would ask more questions in class than anyone else, and that they would pretty much all be simple ones. But he scored so high on a graduate exam that he was accused (falsely) of cheating.[25] The reason other people in his classes kept quiet while he was raising his hand all the time was not because they were smarter than him or that they understood it all already. They just wouldn't consider, or couldn't see, that they didn't understand, or they didn't care to find out. I've seen the same thing many times in classes and engineering work, and the best teachers know the questions to ask in order to demonstrate to everyone that they *don't* grasp as much as they think. Asking those simple questions that expose our ignorance, and even our ignorance of our ignorance, was one thing that Socrates was known for. In

---

[24] Leo Tolstoy, *War and Peace*, vol. 4, part 1, chapter 15.

[25] Cheating on a cumulative test of everything you've ever learned in a subject could only happen if the administrator wouldn't notice a stack of textbooks on the desk, and if you had several days instead of hours to finish it.

general, whatever understanding is, we don't have it, even in science, and we usually fail to even recognize our lack.

And this deficiency is not due to a choice that we make; regardless of whether we are arrogant or humble. Our inability to understand is due to an inherent limitation in our nature. The mathematician Kurt Gödel (widely recognized to have been a genius) agreed, saying that "we have no absolute knowledge of anything. There are degrees of evidence; ...everything goes only by probability." One author paraphrases Gödel's view to be that "we overestimate the clearness of our perceiving."[26] Plenty of other people would also agree that human beings don't truly possess knowledge, and I could quote a lot more of them. But the question that remains after the fact of our unilluminated condition is established—that would be nice to have some idea of an answer to— would be the basic one, again, of what real understanding is and what it would look like if we did have it.

One hint at an answer to that question, of what understanding is, is the fact that only a being with emotions can know or understand anything. A second hint is to observe that, although smart people have a better chance of being able to grasp some things on some level, genuine knowledge is still not accomplished by the intellect. The grasp that physicists have on laws and logic, for example, allows them to discover things about the universe and to build devices like microwaves and nuclear power plants. But the nature of true knowledge goes beyond the realm determined by intellect, and scientists don't possess that knowledge any more than any other person in the world. This is why wisdom is considered to be a mysterious thing that can be possessed, or missed, equally by people of any age or background.

---

[26] Srecko Kovac, "Gödel, Kant, and the Path of a Science," *Inquiry* 51, no. 2 (April 2008): 156.

Again, an astrophysicist might have studied stars for decades and may know all about their history and progressions, and all the physical principles that make them work. Someone without his brainpower and years of training wouldn't be able to connect the physical processes in order to see what experimental findings meant. But, like everyone else in the world, the astrophysicist does not under*stand* that there is a huge ball of gas and fire suspended out in space. Not he, nor any of the rest of us grasp the fact of an enormous mass of flames out there that makes life possible, or that we can actually look up in the sky and see it there—that it sits at some distance from our home, our mother and father, our job, the places we go, and everything else that we've ever known in life. We do not understand that. It is overwhelming, befuddling, and incredible, and nobody realizes it. This shortcoming in our understanding is obvious, and it is just one of thousands of examples.

To give another hint at what real understanding might be: it's easy to imagine a person walking outside one day, doing nothing in particular, when suddenly his jaw drops and his eyes widen as, unprovoked and all of a sudden, he realizes for the first time that a massive body that we've casually termed, "the sun" is out there burning in space, and that he is living on the surface of the earth. No new information would allow him to actually see what he thought he had known his whole life, and he would not have suddenly become smarter. It would just happen. I think we all recognize that such a sudden realization could occur—or maybe something similar actually has occurred to most individuals. And we probably all realize that a computer, or a person without emotions, could not experience such a thing. Again, only a being with emotions is capable of knowledge or understanding.

More examples—and probably no other method—can give a better idea of what this thing is, and help to demonstrate what it isn't. Another might be the case of a man who may have seen the real brutal nature of the world—that anything is allowed to happen and that there are no moral rules set in the universe that can't be defied, or that, even if there are rules, they can all be broken. He might have come to a complete stop at some point and perceived the magnitude of the mass of thousands of years of pain and sorrows across time and across every country and culture, and that this is the world that we're born into. If he did perceive that, and understood it a little bit, he would not be a passive observer, but would have to feel the meaning of it. If he did *not* feel, he would not have a capacity for knowing it, and could have no idea what it meant any more than a brick would.

It's important to realize that comprehending something means more than just to follow causes, effects, and explanations; like simply following how a car's engine works. The day that I learned that there is a God, I was in a kind of shock and I could not forget it. This happened because I had some appreciation of what it really meant.[27] And other people might have their own example where they realized something in a similar way. There's a final example from the book, *The Killer Angels*, that seems to be illogical, but that also gets at the point:

> He had seen them come out of the trees and begin to march up the slope and when he closed his eyes he could still see them coming...He did not understand it: a mile of men flowing slowly, steadily, inevitably up the long green ground, dying all the while, coming to kill you, and the shell bursts appearing above them like instant white flowers.[28]

Soldiers marching up a hill in a battle is not a complicated scenario. But complicated facts and intellectual hurdles were never the

---

[27] Understanding a thing seems to involve and require an ability to *appreciate* it.

[28] Michael Shaara, *The Killer Angels* (New York: Ballantine Books, 1975), 341-42.

obstacle to understanding in the first place. Nevertheless, he did not under*stand* it.

These experiences hint at what genuine understanding is, and indicate that it seems to be far from within our power to produce or achieve it. It's also obvious from the few strange examples that I can think of, that our shortcoming isn't limited to stars in the sky or weighty events. We don't grasp even simple things that we experience. We don't understand that we are alive, we don't appreciate what it means that people come into existence when they didn't exist before, we don't fully understand what it means that we feel, and we don't understand anything else that exists or happens in life. We typically see and read these things like idiots, or like robots incapable of life. And we have no idea about life overall either. We possess some facts, but we obviously do not appreciate and we do not really understand.

"No one can comprehend what goes on under the sun. Despite all his efforts to search it out, man cannot discover its meaning. Even if a wise man claims he knows, he cannot really comprehend it" (Eccl 8:17).

We Want Certainty

It's clear that we simply do not possess understanding. But it would seem like an easier task for us to possess certainty in life. Certainty doesn't seem to be as abstract as understanding, and it seems like it, at least, might be within our reach. And it would matter for us to have this, because our beliefs are woven through us from top to bottom, and a lot of our happiness depends on how sure of them we are. Before looking at whether we do possess this kind of assurance in life, though, it's important to get a better idea of the gigantic value of certainty.

The reason it's worth talking about

There is a very specific and simple reason that certainty is important and worth talking about, which is that it affects our feelings. Just like understanding, certainty can only be possessed by an emotional being. A computer can have information, just like a person, but it can't actually be sure or unsure if any of it is true. If people are sure or unsure of something, though, that assurance or doubt is attached to a feeling that's impossible for us to miss. David Hume said that the only way we know that we believe something is by feelings. In his words, "The difference between fiction and belief lies in some sentiment or feeling, which is annexed to the latter, not to the former."[29] If we believe something, we can recognize a feeling

---

[29] David Hume, *An Enquiry Concerning Human Understanding* (1748), section V, part 2. (*The Empiricists*, 340)

inside that lets us know we believe it. But if we are unsure, we can sense a much less pleasant sensation inside that lets us know that instead. This is the reason certainty is important to us.

We strive to develop a sure worldview

Every belief that we have can cause feelings in us, because every one of them is subject to doubt. And we are packed full of beliefs. We don't only develop a personal stance about big questions like God and death. We also develop personal beliefs and philosophies about everything we've seen in our lives that we have had to come to grips with. We all struggle through childhood and adolescence to develop a view of the world that can give us some amount of peace and help us to deal with the things we see. If a teenager is shunned by a friend, for example, it's pretty much guaranteed that he will develop a philosophy or a rule for himself, and a new belief, in order to make sense of that experience and to be prepared for similar things in the future. We have all done the same thing; for all of our lives. We hold beliefs about how we should behave in the world, about what other people are, about who we are, and about the attitude we should adhere to. And that list goes on for miles. We start building this mental structure in our youth and we cling to it from that time forward. It's commonly known as a *worldview.*

One theologian compares our set of beliefs to a spider's web. If the web is damaged, "It must be repaired at once. If the center is destroyed, all is lost. The spider is compelled to weave a new web. Meanwhile its very existence is threatened, for the web is the spider's life."[30] We don't recognize the importance of our belief structure to us when everything is working. But anyone who has experienced a thought or event that tore a hole in it has known the world-

---

[30] Lauren King, *The Way You Believe* (Newberg, Oregon: The Barclay Press, 1991), 69.

shattering feeling of that, and of the groping and grasping for a set of ideas to be sure of. When something disturbs us, we'll start re-evaluating old beliefs to see if they're still true, frantically, or almost so—like tying lines back together—and we'll be up late at night in some form of emotional pain until we can figure it out. We will ask ourselves questions about what went wrong with the structure—as if we're engineers pulling on various cables and testing pillars to find the fault—and we will try to find out whether modifications to the old beliefs are called for; just as if we're building a new and stronger web of what's really true and what we're going to believe. We can observe young people doing this right before our eyes. They haven't had time to build a dependable structure yet, strengthened and improved over many years, so they're hard at work doing that. And they're not doing it as a hobby. They're doing it because they must, as all people must.

And our worldview includes more than just our religious doctrines and personal philosophies of life, and it goes beyond anything that could possibly be written in a list of beliefs. It is the structure that our minds are built on. The clearest evidence of this is that we can doubt not only those things which are popularly termed and recognized as "personal beliefs," but that we can doubt everything else as well; although it's hard to describe what "everything else" is exactly.

I learned the depth of our belief structure one day quite a few years ago, at age nineteen, when I found myself in a condition I had never known before that it was possible to be in. I'd experienced doubt before that day, about a lot of things, but, before, there had always been like a platform in my mind that I didn't even know existed, on which everything stood, and that nothing could fall below. Any time I'd had doubts previously that had called the big metaphysical beliefs like God and death into question, the experience was unpleasant, but the platform was still there, and every basic thing that I knew before, I still knew. No particular event caused me to get to a place of doubting *all* of it, and I still went about all my functions normally afterwards, but things were shaken for a while in my thinking after finding that the ground level of solid earth was actually a crust of rock floating on molten rock.

Everyone has this kind belief structure. Ground level is made of things that we all believe and that it never even occurs to anyone to argue or question—things we aren't even aware that we believe. We aren't aware either that those things are important to our functioning, but even this platform is far from being good old solid ground, unshakeable and impermeable.

When those basic things are called into doubt, it would be like the effect of September eleventh on someone who saw it happen. The observer would have known very well before the event that it was physically possible for a plane to hit a building and that there are violent people in the world, but he might still be deeply disturbed by it. He might suddenly become unsure of things he'd believed for decades, even though they had nothing to do with the event or with "religion". "Am I strong at all? Is anyone? Do I know *anything* about life at all? Did anyone know the world was like this? Is it possible to be sure of anything?" "I thought the world was good." These, and other more abstract and nameless doubts about ideas we didn't even know were important to us, could disturb any human being *deeply*....The web begins to tear and the ground starts cracking underneath our homes.

I think those people who experience a traumatic event and simply can't handle it and can't go on functioning might have had their foundation cracked in just this kind of way—they become uncertain of *everything*.

All of this is probably the clearest way to see how much certainty matters to us—in the negative side of it—in the pain that doubt causes. Because our beliefs and views are so foundational to us, having them smashed to pieces, even in the context of regular life, is like having a tray of dishes slammed out of our hands to break on the floor, or like a seven-year-old boy having his bag of marbles swatted out of his hands to scatter across the street. It's not a nice feeling.

Even including the broader picture of our condition in this universe, and even including everything else that might happen to cause hurt in this life—like hunger, working long hours, or being injured physically—the pain of doubt in our own minds is one of our worst afflictions. To go into life believing good things about the world and about God, for example, but then encountering something that brings that all into question is one of the most unpleasant things that can happen to a human being. ...The childlike happiness vanishes, and the brightness in the eye is washed out. Even supposing that something very bad, such as personal injury or the death of a friend, is the cause of our doubts, our grief over that awful event itself might not hurt as much as the shattering of beliefs that it could cause. Certainty matters to us.

Examples

The only way I know of to highlight how deeply our beliefs truly go, and to describe the effect uncertainty has on us in those abstract ways that can't be labeled as doubt about particular beliefs on any particular object, is, again, by examples.

While I was in San Diego doing some engineering a few years ago, a co-worker and I crossed the border to see Mexico. I am by no means fearless, but I've been toughened more than most engineers have been, for sure. I can say, though, that the place we ended up at down in Mexico was rough, and was not where visitors would be recommended to go. I was very glad I had a knife with me and I didn't feel comfortable even walking without looking behind us regularly. The place was a whole different world from the nice one that most of us usually live in.

I had commented to my partner something about it being pretty rough, and a couple other things. But he only said after a few minutes of getting there, simply, "I'm so confused." And he hardly spoke the rest of the time. I'm glad he trusted me enough to say what he was actually experiencing, and I understand what had happened to him, because I've felt it before. A big stick had been thrown through his worldview in the area of the ground level beliefs, and I'm sure it hurt then and for a while afterwards. I expect that he spent that night and successive days trying to repair the web that he thought had been dependable after twenty-five years or so of building.

I've personally dealt with everything that has troubled me, as far as I know, but I have also had some doubts or questions that stuck with me and plagued me for years, like ghosts. Things that have no logical connection to particular beliefs of ours—like simply walking through a dangerous town in a foreign country—and should not affect them one way or another, can still shatter our inner framework. And while it doesn't seem apparent, certainty, or lack of it certainty, is what this is all about. We want and need it, and our lack of assurance is the reason for a lot of our pain in life. That is a fact that I feel a need to keep on repeating in order to communicate its massive importance.

As another example: I heard a woman say once that she had read a particularly tragic and horrible story, and that she was not able to sleep for two nights afterwards. It wouldn't be a wild guess to suppose the reason she was troubled was that she was questioning ideas that she had always thought to be true before, and was desperate to find out what had been wrong with her worldview. It would not be a wild guess to suppose that she was up late trying to make sense of things again: accepting the truth about this world, building it into her worldview, and trying to gain some degree of certainty again.

Similarly, I read a book years ago with an account of what the Japanese did to one American who was captured on Iwo Jima. I was about twenty-three then, and had been through what I already described having been through in life. I had already deliberately set out before to grapple with the worst of reality, but this account still shook me and made me question beliefs about a couple things that I hadn't even held open to question, ever. Those things had been obvious, and I had not arrived at them over-night (or even consciously really,) and I had not just flippantly decided that I guessed I would claim to know them. They had come after a lot of struggle, making them precious. But then, *rip*, the web was torn, and I felt it.

Nothing about the event I read about was logically connected with the things it caused me to question either. If someone had brought the new information that I had read to a classroom and written it on a blackboard, then compared it to the beliefs that were affected, a professor would scratch his head, because there would be no connection that made sense, nor would there be any reason that one should have affected the other. But the heart is not logical and it took about two years before the thing stopped raising its ugly head in my mind and until I got some a firm grip back on that part of the world. And this came just from reading a book. I give my examples because they are what I know, but any adult can think of times the same kind of thing has happened to him or her, and the issue at the heart of it is the same again—certainty; we want it badly.

We all have beliefs that are precious to us, and little do we know how much they are woven through us, or how much we depend on them, until they're called into question. If something that a person sees or hears about doesn't make sense, he has to *make* it make sense in some way. It has to be fit into his understanding and belief structure somewhere—engineering the web. What we believe matters to us and we desperately want to be certain, because uncertainty hurts.

> *There is a mine for silver*
>   *and a place where gold is refined...*
> *Man puts an end to the darkness;*
>   *he searches the farthest recesses*
>   *for ore in the blackest darkness.*
> *Far from where people dwell he cuts a shaft...*
> *He tunnels through the rock;*
>   *his eyes see all its treasures...*
> *But where can wisdom be found?*
> *Where does understanding dwell?*
> *Man does not comprehend its worth;*
>   *it cannot be found in the land of the living.*
> *The deep says, 'It is not in me';*
>   *the sea says, 'It is not with me.'*
> *It cannot be bought with the finest gold,*
>   *nor can its price be weighed in silver.*

-Job 28

Lost in the Universe

I had a history professor in college for a couple classes who was almost more interested in pontificating about life and meaning than in teaching the facts. And we all benefited from that. I remember, more than anything else, one phrase he said repeatedly: "*How do you know who is right*?!"[31] That question haunted me for years, and the way he said it wasn't easy to forget. I could also never forget the time I went to visit him in his office, when he told me about something he had seen that had amazed him. He and I were somewhat familiar with each other from class since we both recognized the other as a person who cared about knowing, and I went to his office one day to talk.

At that meeting Dr. Davis told me that several years earlier a young female student had come to him and said that she believed in the sun god Ra, or something. I don't remember exactly which one, but it was, no kidding, an Egyptian or Mesopotamian god, and he pulled the letter out of his desk that she'd given him describing it. The way the man told me about this was meant to convey something to me, and it wasn't just an anecdote about a strange person. It was a sense of amazement and a recognition of something very, very large in this existence that we are all born into.

---

[31] I don't know of any class in public high school or college where any adult is allowed to share his or her honest thoughts with students or to discuss the most important issues in life. There isn't one. Dr. Davis had been at the college for decades and I heard not long ago that they had put a plaque or a statue of him up on the campus.

As I'll try to communicate in my turn now in writing, that thing he tried to communicate is not just one small detail among others. It's like a forest that we live in but never see because it's everywhere and we're used to it. But sometimes it does stand out to a degree that's hard to miss, like with the girl Dr. Davis ran into, or like with a woman I talked to a couple years ago. This woman told me that she attended "various churches, including Latter Day Saints"—meaning Mormon. She was very intelligent and had actually earned a degree in theology from a top university, but she saw no conflict with her choice, even though central teachings of the Mormons and Christians can't be reconciled (assuming only that there is such a thing as logic). I asked if she realized that the two were not the same religion, but it seemed that she actually could not see that there was a conflict. She was an extreme example as well, but the reach of this thing is not limited to people like her, who may seem to make irrational choices.

Aside from Dr. Davis, I had another professor this first year of college who was also not to be forgotten, and my interactions with him demonstrated it as well. Dr. Gregory taught one of the introductory religion classes and was a syncretist, and also a great storyteller. At one point he was telling a Babylonian story about Enkidu and some other figure in a very emphatic voice, as if he was telling a real-life story to kids who had never heard it before. He told how the one "lived out in the woods and grew up in the wild and used to even run with the herds!" As he described Enkidu running through the wild with the animals Dr. Gregory tilted his head back and gave a big howl in the middle of class, "*aaaooooooohhh!*" What a laugh.

He and I were also familiar from class since I had been the only one to speak up about something I thought was true, and he appreciated that. One day I went to his office as well, and he told me that he had been raised in a conservative house in the Midwest, and had been in seminary to become a pastor years before. He didn't finish seminary. He told me that as he was walking across campus one day he realized, "I don't believe this stuff." I expect that doubt had been building in him for a long time. He told me in his office that he now believed that God had revealed himself to different people in different ways, and that this explained why there were different religions.

I know that I was sincere when I was younger and I did not believe that there was a God. And I have little doubt that Dr. Gregory and the other two people I described were sincere. And this means something. There is a condition that we walk around in all our lives and that we have been breathing since we were born:

We live in darkness.

Dr. Davis had seen it, and had been shocked at it, and had tried to communicate it to me that day. I have also now understood, and have felt it, and sometimes I share his shock. We're used to the way things are in this existence, but we're in an almost unbelievable situation. Think of it. We could ask ourselves or someone else what will happen to us after we die, and most people will *actually* say, "*I don't know.*"

The needle should scratch off the record right there! That's important to realize. It's a very dark world for children to be born into where people would have to say that. And if some (theoretical) properly functioning person heard that answer, "*I don't know,*" he would be stunned that the question would even have to be asked in the first place, and would be further amazed at the answer to it, and at the overwhelming darkness the humans live in all their lives.

We, however, aren't surprised at all by this condition. To us it sounds reasonable. But that's only because we have never known anything else. In ways much more extensive than we realize, we are all like the baby taken from the crib and thrown into a brutal situation that we can't get out of; like the child in the movie *Soldier* who had known only strife and death from the start, so that killing and clawing for survival was normal to him. He was never able to consider that the whole situation was perverse. He was born to that, like we were born to this world. And our perspective is also misshapen from the start.[32]

Try again to consider the fact that almost our entire world silently says, "I don't know if there's a God, I don't know where I'm from, I don't know what this world is about, I don't know if there is a life after, or where I'm going." And even those of us who are confident of answers to some of those things are still far from having true certainty, and there are a thousand other critical issues that we have no idea about.

"I don't know" is one of humanity's most characteristic refrains, and the aspect of our condition that's voiced in that statement could be embodied in a figure and put in the center of a painting of the most sad and tragic type possible; entitled, maybe, *Here are the Humans*. "Someone help us. We are lost here and we do not know."

To admit that we do not know

"Who is right!?" And how do you know *you're* right and everyone else is wrong? They think *they're* right and you're wrong. That really used to get to me when I was younger. I was disturbed after talking to Dr. Davis and I was disturbed after talking the next professor as well, as I so often was then. And most of the reason for the turmoil inside me was that I hadn't accepted yet that our uncertainty in this world is inevitable. There is no way around it. I had not come to grips with the simple fact that it is *not* impossible

---

[32] Thank goodness still, though, that children don't come from a sane world and then get transferred into this one after they reach a certain age. They would have a much harder time enduring the world and getting through it, acting like it was just alright, as we have learned to do.

that my beliefs are wrong. Many people will never reach that point, to be able to realize or admit it.

In a way I personally thought it would have been some kind of failure or betrayal to admit that my beliefs were not a certainty. But there is another reason people typically avoid this admission that everything they believe is not one-hundred percent certain as well—pain. The pain of doubt, and the pain of having your worldview torn. Realizing that we are not the wellspring of certainty is usually not a pleasant thing to experience at first. As King put it,

> To hear that our cherished faith statements are only probable (no matter how high the probability) leaves us with something like the feeling of being in an earthquake. Everything trembles and seems about to crash down on our heads. "Surely you do not mean our faith is not certainty!"[33]

That's how it feels.[34]

Reiteration

There is a truth, and it doesn't change based on anything we do. But, as far as our grasp of truth, we are all uncertain as groups, we are all uncertain individually, and there is very little that we can prove. Because of this, whatever we think to be obvious could be entirely wrong. Indeed, this whole life might in fact be just a bad dream…a terrible dream. Anything is possible. If there is a God, he could make us believe that he's good, even if he isn't, as Descartes theorized for the sake of argument. Or there might not be any such

---

[33] King, 45.

[34] That very unwelcome feeling of an earthquake is why, for example, some physicists acted as if they were in a personal war when new ideas about the physical universe were introduced in the early twentieth century. They had put years of effort and training into the view they had of the world, and challenges to those beliefs were not just an academic issue to them. Doubts were psychologically painful and responses were personal.

thing as "good" to begin with. How do we know that we even have any correct concept of it? It could be, and we don't, and who knows, and we've been wrong before, and there's no way to be sure. That's the way it is for us, and it does not make for the most healthy existence. We do not understand, and to answer the question I posed at the beginning of the chapter: *no*, we do *not* have certainty.

Examples

At this point, continuing with attempts to clarify these ideas starts to feel repetitive to me, but this is a very important issue and there are a very, very large number of people of all ages—liberal and conservative and every other type—that seem to have not even a suspicion that every belief and opinion they hold is not certain knowledge. Because of that, I will continue.

To start the illustrations of our constant doubt with world events, we can say for one thing that it's obvious that for most of the conflicts we've ever gone into, we didn't *know* we should have entered them. Sometimes it might have seemed obvious, and sometimes the doubt was greater than others, but uncertainty was never really absent, and it never will be. We had to take our best guess; as we always do regarding anything in life, big or small, and it would be safe to assume that the men who made the decision to go, or not to go, were up late at night hoping and wondering if they'd decided right. They weren't sure.

I hesitate to even use a familiar or particular example because it might be easy to lose sight of the central fact from putting one tree under a microscope, but the American Civil War also demonstrates it well. It was people who almost all nominally believed in the Christian religion, and who should have seen the same things, and should have been in agreement, that fought it. To us this is familiar and we say, 'Of course. It happened because of this and that.' But we are buried up over our heads and swimming in our own misshapen perspective when we try to explain it with any of the reasons the textbooks give. Consider this again: how could it be *possible* that what was ethically correct could not have been seen and agreed on? Personal selfish motives had a role, but the blindness went beyond that, into thousands who had no selfish personal motives at all, but who *still* couldn't see, and didn't know.

Or, I visited Scotland some years ago and went to a battlefield where the Stewarts fought for Bonnie Prince Charlie. These were men in my family, willing to voluntarily face death for what they thought was right, and it meant something to me to see the place. However, after plugging the glorious trumpet taps and cutting through the standard ignorance, the question is, as always, *why?* And *who knew what was right?* They fought because they wanted to restore what they thought was the true religion, Catholicism, to the land. But they had no more access to genuine sight than any of the rest of us do, or ever have. They were ignorant and blind and basically fought out of ignorance and blindness, as did the men on the other side of it.

Uncertainty isn't limited to conflict either. War may be the most condensed manifestation of our inability to be certain, but it's only one symptom of the root cause. Uncertainty is also the entire fuel for politics. If we actually knew, there wouldn't be any political argument. And is one side enlightened while the other isn't? The individuals that won't recognize any gray, won't recognize that they could be wrong, and won't recognize the inherent doubt in their opinions, are the very most ignorant people. But the normal pattern of thought in comparing one's own opinions to those of another person seems to be something like this: "There is absolutely no ground or validity whatsoever to anything they believe in any way. I know, because I know the answers to these things for certain." It's surprising that in a world where our judgement is so obviously clouded and incomplete, there are so many claims like that. The truth is that any individual or group argues for their best *guess* as to what's true or right. That's all. If we were sure, there wouldn't be political parties.

Prestigious international councils of wise men and institutions shouldn't fool anyone either. We send our best blind men to meet representatives of the other nations of poor ignorant animals. Darkness and uncertainty—that's the correct cause and explanation for almost any conflict there has ever been, and for about half of everything else that happens in human life.

And I should also emphasize again that, although the uncertainty might be most easily exemplified in controversial world events and decision-making by groups of people, no one should think of one time or event as a periodic outbreak of uncertainty in the world—"Gee, I'm glad life isn't usually like that." It is *always* like that, every day, in every thing. The doubt is only more apparent at some times than at others. And it also isn't limited to large groups of people. Like the poster says, an avalanche of destruction is the result of a bunch of harmless flakes working together. Groups are composed of individuals, and individuals in this world live in doubt all their lives. The occasional large scale events just follow along as a result of this basic condition that characterizes every person every day.

No one is immune

This darkness in our species is so obvious and inevitable that it seems to be a characteristic of the human creature like being migratory is a characteristic of geese. Geese are migratory, have long necks, and eat a diet primarily of vegetation. Humans give birth to live young, eat a varied diet, and spend their lives in darkness and uncertainty. No one is immune to it. We're all hesitant; we might be wrong; we've sure been wrong a thousand times before, and no one should suppose that any human being is above this. There is no one who wouldn't ever have cause to ask himself, "Is it really true? And *am* I really right where others are wrong?" Everyone has been wrong before, and darkness applies to all: the Hindus and Muslims, Atheists, Christians, Buddhists, Shinto, the ridiculous cults, and the complacents. Unless those people are inherently different types of creatures and not part of the homo sapien species, they don't have any more unshakeable knowledge than anyone else.

A particular point should also be made to say that the man of science and reason, confident that there is not a God, doesn't know that what he believes is true any more than the theist. He is no empiricist and rational machine where the other is a believer. He doesn't know if there's a God who made the whole universe and directs all things, or not. He is another blind animal that has to trust that his conclusions on what is most probable are correct.

I'll take the time to point out specifically also that Christians are not immune to the human condition. Even if the Bible is true, and a person believes it, he is still mostly blind and uncertain about life in general. Behavior throughout history demonstrates that unequivocally. If there was certainty, there wouldn't have ever had to be struggle between honest people to resolve interpretations and doctrinal issues. But that struggle existed from the very beginning. Or, John the Baptist is a good example of doubt in Christians. The account says that he saw the Holy Spirit descend on Jesus with his own physical eyes and that God had spoken to John, telling him who God-on-earth would be when he saw him. Nevertheless, after all that, when John was in prison he sent his disciples to ask Jesus if he was really the one. It's clear that John wasn't certain after all; or, at least, that his certainty didn't last. But we *are* certain? We should make some effort to be more realistic.

I still do not mean to say that no one *should* be sure, or that no one *should* have an impermeable confidence forever. I, for example, would be a colossal sucker to doubt several things after what I've seen and learned. And, indeed, the things people believe may very well be true, and it may be that, given a particular set of evidence, we *should* be one-hundred percent certain of particular beliefs in life. But we just aren't. That's not how we work, and that is not the way that things are for us here in this existence[35]

Even if we are right, we don't know it

We're not sure. And another point to recognize is that even if those people who are confident that they're right are indeed correct, and their beliefs are true where all others are false...they still don't know that! Even when people *are* right, there is still not certainty. Xenophanes said, "No man knows or will ever know about the gods and the other things I speak of; For even if one happened to speak the whole truth, He himself would not know it. All things are wrought with appearance."[36] Someone might happen to be correct, but he will not be completely sure that he is. We may have a very high degree of confidence that we are right, and we may indeed *be* right, but we do *not* know that.[37] The doubt remains.

Conclusion

In conclusion, our minds and our knowledge are absolutely not so solid. They do not rest on some immovable internal ground. I realized on my day lying on the floor when I was nineteen, that everyone lives by their best guess on many things—probabilities in even the most minute detail, every day, all the time, in every

---

[35] King—who is an evangelical theology professor—supports this fact, "No one raises an eyebrow over the proposition that hypotheses are tentative until tested and verified. This is inherent in the scientific process. Hypotheses are about matters not yet thoroughly known. But if hypotheses and faith statements are fundamentally alike, then we must consider the idea that faith statements are also tentative, probable, not absolutely certain" (King, 45).

[36] Xenophanes, I.16 fr. 34. (Ancient, 21)

[37] I believe that there are moments when we possess complete certainty, but that these are rare. See the succeeding chapter "Conclusion on Knowing."

imaginable area. We wonder what to do about someone we associate with. We don't know if they are right or we are. We don't know if something we're doing is appropriate to the situation, we don't know if something is wrong with our heart and personality, or what caused it. We can't decide about even regular daily issues, and when we do we are rarely sure of the accuracy of what we choose. No one lives or does anything except by relying on the tentative assurance they have of everything that they think they know. This is the case in metaphysics and in daily life. Except for a few rare moments, we do not have certainty in life.

What it means

Having pointed this out now, I'd like to interpret what it means, and to take a step back and reflect on our situation in broader terms; to put our uncertainty into context so that we might have a chance of appreciating where we are.

Consider again that we really have no idea, but that we somehow *live* this way. And consider what a sane and proper perspective of that fact would be. What would be the correct way to feel about our condition? I think it's clear that if we could view our condition without the illusion of normality that we ascribe to it, we would react with the same kind of shock that Dr. Davis did, or that Pascal did. Pascal describes:

> When I see the blind and wretched state of man, when I survey the whole universe in its dumbness and man left to himself with no light, as though lost in this corner of the universe without knowing who put him there, what he has come to do, what will become of him when he dies, incapable of knowing anything, I am moved to terror, like a man transported in his sleep to some terrifying desert island, who wakes up quite lost and with no means of escape. Then I marvel that so wretched a state does not drive people to

despair. I see other people around me, made like myself. I ask them if they are any better informed than I, and they say they are not.[38]

The meaning and impact of our perpetual uncertainty becomes clearer when viewed from a reasonable perspective such as Pascal's, but it becomes clearer yet when put into the broadest context, which is the nature of this universe in general. If we keep it within our view what the rest of our living conditions are really like in this world, then the shocking fact of our lifelong doubt seems to fit right in there; like a final insult.[39]

As any adult knows, the wider context for our situation is that we live in an existence where anything can happen (and not only *can* it happen, but it already *has*), and that it is bad beyond comprehension. The things that happen in any place, characterize that place for what it is. If parents knew, for example, that children at a particular daycare were regularly maimed, murdered, abused, and turned out with debilitating illnesses, they would correctly declare that location to be perverse and horrible; not fit for anyone to live in. So the question to ask is this: what would be a correct and reasonable declaration on the nature of *this* universe and existence that we all live in, where those exact things, and worse, happen every day? It would be the same as for the daycare — that this world and existence is perverse, horrible, and not fit for anyone to live in.

We make the best of things, and we look on the positive side in life. And this is indeed the wisest attitude to have. Wonderful

---

[38] Blaise Pascal, *Pensees* XV, 198 H5. (p 59).

[39] I should say maybe that I'm not deliberately trying to make people want to jump off buildings. There are a lot of good things in this world too. And it makes no sense at all to dwell on the bad. But what's true is true. Describing reality doesn't make it any different. But describing a problem and taking an honest look at our situation can actually be helpful for our emotions and mental well-being, such as it is.

and beautiful things do exist here and can happen here. But that still doesn't mean the nature of this place is good. The fact that a child was tied up, doused with gasoline, and lit on fire by another kid, gives the lie to that fantasyland belief, and anyone from a decent universe who was suddenly transported here to ours would be able to see things for what they really are, and he would be horrified. If he saw or heard of a bad car accident or one of the innumerable other terrors that our world features daily, or if he simply heard of the simple facts of our daily existence, he would be in shock, and would probably stop himself within just a couple minutes and conclude that he was having a nightmare. It would seem too insane to be real. We, however, could assure him that it is all too real. And maybe we could give him the brochure, "Welcome to our universe…motto and trademark: '*Where the suffering has no limit!*'"[40]

That is the broader context of the world we live in. And with that in view, it doesn't seem quite as shocking that, *in addition* to physical suffering and death, we live in doubt all of our living days, and that we cannot see. It seems to fit right in like a cherry on top, or like a final punch to the kidney. *We do not know.* We don't know where we're going when we die, how we got here, what this place is about, what absolute moral line divides all things, or if there even is one, or what we should do. And even if God did tell us answers, or

---

[40] It should be understood as well, by the way, that this would not be the brochure only for planet Earth. The nature of this life would still be the same if we inhabited some other planet in a distant galaxy. A warp drive powered hover truck in our distant and "better" world could still maim a child for life, for example, with no explanation or apology offered from the universe. All the things that happen here, could still happen there. And even if we stopped all of them somehow, the fact that they *could* happen, and *would* if we couldn't prevent it, is what defines the nature of this existence. And that nature is *not* good. Our future world wouldn't change that; it would still be brutal, perverse, and horrifying. Likewise for our darkness—we wouldn't be any more certain of answers to any questions in some supposed utopia in another galaxy than we are here; as long as the nature of this life is still what it is now. The only one who can change it is God.

if he already has, our nature would not allow us to trust them completely. In this place there is almost never any certainty of anything. And this darkness doesn't only apply when earth shaking events have to be considered, but it is always with us. We live in it every day, all the time, in every issue. The magnitude of it is shocking. *Here are the Humans*; we do not understand, and we do not possess certainty.[41]

"See, darkness covers the earth and thick darkness is over the peoples" (Isaiah 60:2).

---

[41] I'll add here at the end that, despite the fact of our impermeable uncertainty, there are a huge number of people who don't care to know the truth anyway, and who consciously repress certain truths from themselves because of the implications those things would have on their lives. The facts of our uncertainty in this world will not excuse that behavior.

Certainty in Science & Philosophy

We are lost in the world, or, at best, we've built a weak, frail web that we depend on, but in which we can't have much confidence. It has proven to be wrong, incomplete, or fragile many times before, so we can almost never be truly certain of anything we believe. This is the way it has always been. In the realm of religious questions, and of life, we know nothing. But, amazingly, there's another realm in which we *are* certain! Science. Things go differently for us there.

In 1637 Pierre Fermat wrote in the margin of a book he was reading, that he had figured out a proof for the mathematical statement that no three positive integers a, b, and c can solve the equation $a^n + b^n = c^n$ for any value of n greater than two. This theorem was very important to mathematicians, and they tried to prove it for hundreds of years without success, until someone came through around 1995. Amir Aczel describes the situation,

> No one ever believed it would be proven in our lifetime. The theorem was so difficult, and so many people had tried to prove it for over three hundred years. We were well aware that entire branches of mathematics had been developed as the result of attempts to prove the theorem.

But the attempts failed, one by one. Fermat's Last Theorem had come to symbolize the unattainable.[42]

But then a really smart guy succeeded, finally. Aczel describes: "Headlines in the world's newspapers hailed the unexpected breakthrough. 'At Last, Shout of 'Eureka' In Age-Old Math Mystery' announced the front page of the *New York Times* on June 24, 1993."[43]

Another scientific question that has been more meaningful to most people than the math thing, and that also demonstrates the point that shouldn't be missed, is the question of what the planets are and how they move. From the time we first looked at the sky at night we could tell that the planets weren't the same thing as the stars because they don't always come above the horizon at the same time, and they don't stay in the same place in relation to all the stars in the sky. After many centuries of not knowing what we lived on and what the lights up there were, and what this whole thing was in general that we had been deposited in, we were able to figure out, at least, that the wandering lights moved around the sun as the earth does. But we still couldn't tell how they moved. It didn't add up that they followed circular paths, and we couldn't figure that question out for centuries. But, finally, in 1605 Johannes Kepler discovered that the planets trace out an ellipse in space rather than a circle. It was a breakthrough and another step forward in sure knowledge.

Science is not the same

Regarding Fermat's Theorem, most people would say "who cares and so what" but the point to notice was that something very

---

[42] Amir Aczel, *Fermat's Last Theorem*, (New York: Four Walls Eight Windows, 1996), preface, vii.

[43] Aczel, 4.

important to a group of people was unknown, and that it defied proof for generations, but it was then solved at last, and for good. And what should also be noticed about the question of the planets was that after a very long time of questioning and theories, both childish and intelligent, someone finally came through and the great question was solved; at long last. Let every creature rejoice, we finally found the answer.

We also figured out what disease is—that the unknown killers that inflicted suffering on the entire globe and wiped out wives, children, villages, and families were caused by tiny animal things—and we learned how to fight them. We figured out what everything solid in the world is made of as well.[44] We figured out what *light* is, and how to work with it in all kinds of incredible ways. We figured out a lot of things, and all of these examples represent the way it has been in science from the start. We have *made* advancements. And for most of the biggest ones, what happened was that a gifted person was born, that person went to work, and that person furthered our knowledge unequivocally by building on work that had been done before. The race strode bravely forward in knowledge.

That is how it has gone, and there might truly be nothing that we can't discover in science. Time after time we accomplish things and learn things that had been considered impossible before. As Hume put it,

> The motive of blind despair can never reasonably have place in the sciences, since, however unsuccessful former attempts may have proved, there is still room to hope, that the industry, good fortune, or improved sagacity of succeeding

---

[44] Or so we think.

generations may reach discoveries unknown to former ages.[45]

We just might make a time machine or a warp drive one day. And I'm not trying to be funny there. It could happen. We also just might discover the graviton and find answers to whatever else we wonder about in the physical world.

But things are definitely not like that in metaphysics and religion. In metaphysics we get precisely *nowhere* and we have gotten there with perfect consistency for thousands of years! There is a huge and distinct difference between the realm of science and the realm of religious questions. Immanuel Kant points this out in the preface to his *Prolegomena for any Future Metaphysics*:

> If metaphysics is a science, why is it that it cannot, as other sciences attain universal and lasting acclaim? If it is not, how does it happen that, under the pretense of a science it incessantly shows off, and strings along the human understanding with hopes that never dim but are never fulfilled?...It seems almost laughable that, while every other science makes continuous progress, metaphysics, which desires to be wisdom itself, and which everyone consults as an oracle, perpetually turns round on the same spot without coming a step further.[46]

Another author also comments that "the juxtaposition of science and math with metaphysics and religion is obvious. In math problems can be solved."[47] In math, problems can be solved; in metaphysics/religion, they *can't* be solved. That's the way it looks.

---

[45] Hume, *Enquiry*, section I, ~p 5. 312.

[46] Immanuel Kant, *Prolegomena to Any Future Metaphysics*, (1783), preface, 5-6.

[47] Torkel Franzen, "The Popular Impact of Gödel's Incompleteness Theorem," *Notices of the American Mathematical Society*, 2006, 441.

Who has any hope that if we just put our minds to it and get our best people working on the problem, we can figure out *life* or religion?

Our confidence that we can continue to figure out physical things such as those involving biology, matter, and space, is proved by the tons of money we spend on scientific research. The space program is not cheap. The gigantic telescopes aren't cheap and neither are the particle accelerators or biology labs or the salaries of all the people who design and run those things. But we pay for it because we are confident that advancement will be made; answers will be found.

However, for some reason we do *not* fund research into the *important* questions, such as where our children, who are all doomed to death, will be going! Not one nickel. And that is amazing. Why is it that we don't even try? The reason is that even the idea that we could make any kind of progress in religion as we do in science is preposterous to us. We seem to know better than to hope; by instinct apparently. Possible newspaper headlines such as, "The Washington State religious research group has made new advancements…" or, "The philosophy department of Georgetown University has recently proved in their state of the art facility that the soul is…" They don't add up. For some reason the idea that any kind of definite progress in knowledge of life or religion could be made is actually like a joke to us. Nobody expects there to be any religious truth that can be proved by any tool of logic, reason or experiment.

I think our awareness of history explains a lot of this. In our history there has always been a vast and obvious gap between metaphysics and science. It has existed from the start, whether we recognized that gap from the start or not.

Philosophy is the field that tries to answer religious questions, and all other questions, by logical analysis and argument—the very same tools that scientists use. Philosophy has also tried to consider itself a science, but this has never seemed to work. It seems to have turned out that one guy's guess is as good as another's in all of the important questions of metaphysics, whereas, in the physical sciences, and in mathematics, the truth is known, and real advancements are made. This was one thing that attracted me to science in the first place—what's true is true and no one can argue it. Faith is not required. That appealed to me as a nineteen year old in a university surrounding of varying opinions and relativism, and after I had known very, very well the pain of doubt.

In philosophy and religion, one guy says one thing and another guy says something else. Everyone capable of speech has some half-baked opinion. The famous philosophers are not fools, but none of them could do anything more than argue either. Plato describes the cave and the shadows and the soul, but another guy says that's wrong, then another philosopher says what the other guy said is wrong, in two-hundred pages of words, and gives an argument about language not correlating to ideas, etc. The next guy says language is truly inherent in the human being, then the next says there is no soul and that everything is experience and habit. And the lips go flappity-flap one century after another without any agreement or any proof of a single thing.

We haven't had any success, but we *have* tried

Unlike science, no resolution or final answer in metaphysics has ever happened, although the failure is certainly not for lack of trying. Some of our very brightest have put their very best efforts into finding these answers since ancient times. As one example, people have attempted to prove logically and methodically that there is a God. But the supposed proofs have probably never actually convinced anyone, including the individuals who derived them, and none that I've ever seen has made much sense.

Anselm's (1033-1109 A.D.) was the first popular one, by the way, and it is still the most famous. Anselm was a theologian and his argument is known as the "Ontological Argument."

Philosophers and theologians are still debating whether it's valid. It goes like this: we can all have an idea of the greatest possible thing that there could be; so that idea exists. And this thought or idea is of an infinite God. But anyone would agree that something that actually exists in the real world (not just in the mind) is greater than something that exists only in the mind. So there's supposed to be a contradiction if God *didn't* exist because a chair or anything else that existed in the real world would be greater than our idea of him...but everyone had agreed that God was the greatest possible thought. Hence, the contradiction, supposedly. I don't think there's a real contradiction, but some people do.[48] The whole thing, though, is more humorous than convincing. It was a good try, but the argument really doesn't help anyone, and the human race's perfect record of zero progress was clearly maintained.

As another example, Rene Descartes (maybe one of the most intelligent people to have ever lived) had three proposed proofs of God's existence. One of them was similar to Anselm's and was also based on the fact that we all have a concept of an eternal and infinite God. It's a fact that we have this infinite idea, even though we are all finite and severely limited. So, being finite, there is no way that we ourselves could even conceive of this, nor create this idea that we possess. Only an infinite being beyond us could create even the thought of God, since the thought itself is beyond the ability of finite beings to come up with.[49] The reasoning is not bad, but no one agrees on this argument or any other one.

---

[48] The other disputants to the argument are also not just obstinate atheists. The first objection to Anselm came from a monk. And Thomas Aquinas (sainted by the Catholic church) didn't think the argument was valid.

[49] Rene Descartes' was a very pious man and it's clear from reading his work that he had an intelligence like a top-fuel drag car. The degree of his intelligence is especially obvious in his responses to critics. It was probably clear to them after reading his replies that he was in a league of his own. He also was not a geek-boy who wouldn't have been able to hang out with men. He had been a soldier in his youth and most biographers comment that he seemed to love the soldier's life.

These attempts do carry some weight and do mean something, but no one can say whether they are proofs or not. I would bet several thousand also that even Descartes was less than convinced. Pascal had the same opinion, saying that arguments like these are

> so remote from human reasoning and so involved that they make little impact, and, even if they did help some people, it would only be for the moment during which they watched the demonstration, because an hour later they would be afraid they had made a mistake.[50]

He also said that "We have an incapacity for proving anything which no amount of dogmatism can overcome,"[51]

And Pascal's analysis is right on. In metaphysics we get nowhere. In religion we get nowhere. We can't answer the most important questions and we don't even make any progress (outside of things that can be empirically studied—not many people are worshipping the sun now, but only because we can study it physically now and see what it is). But there is no such fiasco in math or science. There are actual proofs there, and those who can't see that they are proofs just aren't smart enough to grasp them and they shouldn't be in the field.[52] Opinion or personal belief has nothing to do with it.

Mathematics depends on logic, and physics depends on logic and experiment. Concepts of physics are proven by experiment and our ability to interpret what we observe. Those who can't cut it to see the correct interpretation are *out*. They don't know what

---

[50] Pascal, XIV Excellence of This Means of Proving God, paragraph 190. (57).

[51] Pascal, paragraph 406 (from unclassified papers). (119).

[52] There are other fields like systems engineering, for example, that require almost no intelligence. Maybe I should have gotten in there since the real science was so hard for me.

they're doing and they don't have the brainpower to see what's been shown, and there are no two ways about that. People who have no idea what they're talking about can be conclusively ignored in science. In metaphysics, though, anyone can babble indefinitely and can never be proved wrong, even if they have never seriously considered anything, or even if they are deliberately obstinate or insincere.

That is how it has always gone with efforts in metaphysics compared to those in science.

What limits us?

Imagine, though, if the question of whether God exists was answered for certain, or if someone proved that we will continue on after death, and proved what that next life would be. And imagine that the knowledge of those answers spread around the world like findings in science always have—with unanimity, except for a handful of crackpots that could be easily dismissed. Answering those questions definitively would change the world and the way human beings have always been. But this has never happened. Not a single question has ever been answered. Not once in thousands of years.

Why?

Why exactly *is* it that advancement is possible in science but apparently impossible in metaphysics?[53] The question deserves to be asked a thousand times!

---

[53] Although, there is no reason the question of whether we live on after the body dies should be a "religious" question. It is a completely sound and logical question just like the one of what matter is composed of. Both are equally valid. The one on death is only "religious" because it has defied answer and probably will never yield results to empirical experiment.

Part of the answer might be hinted at in an article I read ten years ago in *Discover* magazine. The mathematician Thomas Hale proposed a proof of "Kepler's 390 year-old conjecture that the most efficient way to pack equal-size spheres (such as cannonballs on a ship—which is how the question arose) is to stack them in the familiar pyramid fashion." Hale waited five years for any kind of verdict of approval to his submission. The article said that

> After examining Hale's argument for five years, in the spring of 2003 a review panel of world experts appointed by the prestigious journal *Annals of Mathematics* finally declared that, whereas they had not found any irreparable error in the proof, they were still not sure that it was correct. The journal agreed to publish Hale's proof, but only with a disclaimer saying they were not sure that it was right.[54]

Why couldn't the wise men figure out whether the proof was correct, and agree about it? What limited them from success? I'm confident that the element lacking was pure *brainpower*. Brainpower is what has always overcome problems in science. That's what Kepler had that enabled him to figure out the elliptical orbits of the planets, where others couldn't. Tycho Brahe had compiled all the data, but he wasn't as smart as Kepler, so he wasn't able to put it all together. Gauss, DeBroglie, Einstein, Newton, and Euclid were also geniuses and, as for Kepler, it was because of the strength of their intelligence compared to that of other people that they could do what others couldn't. It was a matter of degree— having *enough* of something. And the issue of figuring out the mathematical proof is the same, I think. Most of us can't even see much easier proofs, whereas smarter people can see them clearly. But it turns out that the very smartest people have limits also, of

---

[54] Keith Devlin, "Mathematicians Face Uncertainty," *Discover* 25, no. 1 (January, 2004): 36.

course, and it seems that the cannonball proof is an example of that. The frontier of knowledge in science and math is conquered by brains, hard work, and logic. And our weakness in those things is what limits us there. Maybe there is something similar that limits us in metaphysics.

If the element that limits us from furthering our knowledge in this metaphysics was also brainpower, though, as it is in science, it would seem that we would have at least figured out one or two things over these thousands of years. The stacked cannonballs was a very difficult scenario as it turned out, and we were too limited to figure that one out for sure. But we have figured out thousands of simpler things in science. And some comparably simple things do also exist in metaphysics; like Anselm's or Descartes' argument for the existence of God. Again, it would seem like we should be able to figure out at least a couple of them! However, we haven't been able to definitively evaluate the truth or falsehood of those or any others.

> It is the degree of our intelligence that limits us in science.
> *What is it that limits us in metaphysics?*

At this point we might begin to suspect that it's something that we simply do not have, rather than something we don't have *enough* of.

How Could We Find Certain Answers in Religion

When things are good, people very rarely care about answers to religious questions, and if the world was good and people didn't die, we might never care at all and our uncertainty might not matter much. Looking into death and God then might be like a treasure hunt, as if set up for our amusement. But our real condition is precarious, with some kind of doom just around the corner for every single person and everyone they care about. And this makes our uncertainty cause pain in life, and fear at death, even for those who are confident of what they believe, since no one is immune to doubts.

Our situation, then, makes finding answers something more than amusement, and it makes metaphysics something more than just an esoteric hobby of some dry nerds.[55] It is critically important for all of us to know answers. This is why I am concentrating on providing any kind of answers that I can, and why I'm presenting every kind of question that can be asked; because it matters.

I concluded the last chapter by asking what keeps us from making progress in religion as we have in science. I think that a specific answer to that is impossible. But before asking the question

---

[55] I hesitated to even use the word metaphysics to describe these questions because it might give that impression.

in that way, it should be asked in a different way—in a positive form. The question is this:

> If we are going to discover answers to religious questions that everyone will agree on, how could it happen? What tool or ability do we have that could make that possible, so that we could make advancement in metaphysics as we have in science?

This should be addressed first.

Fortunately, our history can tell us what will probably *not* ever allow us to make progress in metaphysics. The experience of our whole race in pursuing solutions to the important questions is like a millennia long statistical trial—the greatest and most well-documented trial of all time. And one of the findings of that trial is that if God does exist, he does not let anyone touch, see, or hear him (hardly ever), or detect him by any other physical sense. The multi-thousand-year long trial has revealed that conclusion, at least. Similarly, we can conclude from experience that we will probably never be finding out whether we have an immortal soul by slicing people into samples to put under the microscope, or by any other physical means. The experience of our species has shown that probably *none* of the metaphysical questions that we care about most will be answered through physical detection or analysis; which is fitting since *metaphysics* actually means "beyond the physical."

Physical experiment won't get us our answers. And another thing that would never work would be for one person to find answers and then tell everyone else. Particular individuals might experience events that they believe to be revelations from God, and they might be sure of their beliefs from that time forward, but the race will never take the word of one person, and will never reach any agreement based on the word of any individual; for very good reason. Many people also might believe that God has revealed answers in one way or another, such as in feelings we get from nature, or in some kind of code in the universe, but humanity as a whole will never agree on that either. None of these possibilities could allow us to find answers. So how could we ever make progress in curing our uncertainty and finding answers to the important questions?

The only tool of discovery left to us if bigger microscopes, more powerful particle accelerators, and farther reaching rocket ships won't work, is going to be one of the mind. But if we aren't going to trust in the mind of any one individual who claims to have exerted his spirit, emotions, moral force, or any other personal mental capacity to discover truths, then the only mental capacity or tool that might theoretically allow us to advance would have to be something common to all people and that can be demonstrated to all people. It would have to be something that would allow one person to lay out the evidence to another and say, "see for yourself," so that the second person could then use the same tool that everyone else has, turn the crank, and watch it measure the stuff up to be true or false.

Feelings don't work that way and personal conviction of truth doesn't work that way. The only tool that has ever met those conditions is *logic*. It is the only ability we have that has ever allowed the human species to make definite unequivocal progress in abstract knowledge, and it happens to be the same tool responsible for all of our scientific advancement as well. Without it we never could have done so much as put two and two together, and we still wouldn't be able to. So, unless God pulls back the veil, the only way that we could find answers and advance in religion/metaphysics, as we have so many times in science, would be by logical argument.

When logic and reason (which are the same thing really) are applied correctly, they cannot be argued with by anyone. Or, if someone does argue, that person can easily and accurately be dismissed as being either crazy or incompetent. If we are told that a coin with a head and tails is flipped and that it doesn't land on heads, logic kicks in to let us see that the coin landed on tails. There is no question about it and personal opinion or belief has nothing to do with it; thank goodness. Only quacks deny that momentum is conserved, light is quantized, the derivative of sine is cosine, or any of those other things we've grasped by this tool. Anything can and will be argued, *except logical proof.* So this tool is our one hope of curing uncertainty.

As Hume put it,

> Accurate and just reasoning is the only catholic [universal] remedy, fitted for all persons and all dispositions; and is alone able to subvert that abstruse philosophy and metaphysical jargon, which, being mixed up with popular superstition, renders it in a manner impenetrable to careless reasoners, and gives it the air of science and wisdom.[56]

I.e., reason or logic is the only thing that could ever clear up all the guesswork and trash, and it is the only thing that would be a "catholic remedy"—that would have to be agreed on by any sane or rational person regardless of where or when he or she is from or what they believe.

Conclusions reached using logic are the only ones that everyone could ever be—or have ever been—agreed on. And there is a reason that it works so well. As Hume also said, "The faculties of the mind are supposed to be naturally alike in every individual; otherwise nothing could be more fruitless than to reason or dispute together."[57] What this means is that if some people had a tool of the mind that was a type A, and other people had a tool type B, and the tools worked differently and gave different answers, it wouldn't do

---

[56] Hume, Enquiry, section 1, p 5. (p 313).

[57] Hume, VIII Of Liberty and Necessity, part 1. (364)

any good for the people in the different groups to reason together. The different tool they had access to would give different answers, and there could never be agreement. However, the faculties of the mind *are* the same in all sane human beings, and this is why conclusions arrived at through reason are communicated so easily and unanimously across culture, ethnicity, or any other difference imaginable (except maybe gender).

If a guy in India has a chemical analyzer and he measures some sample with it, the verdict it gives him will be the same that it gives a guy in Bolivia, China, or France who is using the same model of analyzer. This is why there is essentially always unanimity in Physics and math—everyone is using the same tool to determine truth—logic—and it works the same in everyone. This "faculty" is "alike in every individual."

There's unanimity in things that answer to logic, and if religious answers were arrived at in this way, by real proofs, the papers listing the proofs would be in every journal and sent to educated people around the world first, just like they have been in science for generations. Every country's self-respecting people of science would get the findings, then word would get to the government, and before long it would be a major embarrassment for anyone to deny the answers, no matter what their culture or values. No group or nation wants to look backward, ignorant, or obstinate. That's one other thing the whole world agrees on even now. To deny real proofs, even in religious issues, would be like denying that the earth revolves around the sun—again, a real embarrassment. There would be unanimity.

If we could answer religious questions with logical proofs, *then* we would make progress. And this is the summary: Logic is the only avenue that could advance the human race in knowledge of religious questions. And what all of this means, then, is that to ask "what limits us in metaphysics?" is the same as to ask, "what is the limit of logic? How far can it be used?"

The limit of logic is also the limit of the progress humanity can make in curing our uncertainty.

The potential of logic

Basically all of America's founding fathers were children of the Enlightenment, and we are very lucky for that. The human race has always been in darkness, and it still is now, but it used to be even darker and stupider. For millennia we groped about, knowing almost nothing. But when humans began to see the power of reason our poor race latched onto it like a lifeboat arriving after thousands of years lost out at sea. "At last we have light! *All hail logic!*" After eons of darkness, plagues, and ignorance, we found something that provided some real cures and some real answers. It was proven to work, and were not foolish to value it above gold.

It has enabled us to do a huge amount of discovery and good since we first began to appreciate it, and the world has been very enthusiastic for just how far reason and its application (i.e., science) can take us. Apparently Gottfried Leibniz had a vision of a world where the reach of reason was extended much farther, to solve even more problems than it has today. His vision voices our own hopes and the hopes of western society pretty well. He put his finger on this bright expectation for how far reason can take the species, where to us it is a vaguely felt anticipation. Berlinski summarized Leibniz's vision using an imagined conversation of Leibniz with his patron, where he proposes a universal language of symbols that covers *everything*:

"If we had it...we would be able to reason in metaphysics or morals in much the same way as in geometry and analysis. If controversies were to arise, there would be no more need of disputation between two philosophers than between two accountants. For it would suffice to take their pencils in hand, sit down to their slates, and to say to each other (with a friend as witness, if they liked): 'Let us calculate.'"[58]

Imagine—even moral debates resolved by logic, with certainty! Who can now say what is the "right" view of immigration, war, welfare, and all those other things we argue about? No one *knows*, and no one can prove anyone else to be wrong. Everything is just personal opinions and our best guess. But if logic could be extended like Leibniz envisioned, we would be living in a different world.

"Should it ever be allowed for prisoners to be drugged or otherwise pressured in an effort to protect our people?"

"...Let us calculate."

"Should we intervene militarily in this African civil war?"

"...Let us calculate."

"Why is the world like this?"

"The calculations have told us _____."

"Is there a God?" "Is there a heaven?"

"We have calculated and the answer is _____."

That is what it would be like if logic could work in metaphysics like it does in science. And no one could doubt the proofs. Our uncertainty in life and the pain that it causes us would begin to be healed. It is a wonderful possibility.

---

[58] Berlinski, 12.

Does Reason Exist?

If you're crossing the ocean in a ship, you can't jump out and decide to go on your own. You will go only as far as the ship can take you. The only way you can leave it is if another ship appears that you can transfer to. But in humanity's search for answers in metaphysics we have exactly one ship, and there is nothing else anywhere in sight. Logic is it. This fact, and the possibility of Leibniz's incredible dream for how far logic could take us, makes it critical to know that there really is such a thing as reason/logic, and makes it advisable for us to do everything we can to try to understand its nature.

The possibility that reason doesn't really exist, or that it's just an illusion, does not seem like such a ridiculous idea after reading David Hume's work. To mention a little more about him than just his name: David Hume (Scottish, 1711-76) was one of the first to stop and look down in his hand at this thing that had been used and trusted for so long through the Enlightenment and before, and to ask if it was really the cure-all for humanity. Leibniz had lived in a time when it seemed that reason could do anything, and he is usually the character chosen to represent that view. But Hume questioned it.

Logic works on necessity: the coin didn't land on heads, and it only has a heads and tails, so it must have landed on tails. Triangle ABC equals triangle BDA, therefore by necessity... The oil drops deflect different amounts under a field, therefore...

Everything we figure out in science and math and many other areas of life are figured out by logic. But according to Hume, nothing is necessary based on anything else, as far as we know. And if he is right it would be a big problem for the reality and the power logic. What Hume's statement about necessity means is that all circumstances and events are just what happens, and the supposed cause and effect that we think we see is just our own experience pasted onto the universe like a fake label, to help make us feel like we understand things.

According to Hume, we don't put together that one thing must logically follow from some other set of facts; we only think we are able to do that. In reality, what's happening is that the animal brain has seen things happen enough times that it observes cause and effect, cause and effect, like Pavlov's dog drooling because it hears the bell and has experienced enough times that food is coming. A bell ringing doesn't logically require that food will appear, but the dog might think that very thing, in his own way. A very smart philosopher dog might say to himself: "The sound of the bell shakes food out of the ether of space...makes perfect sense." He would think the food's arrival was necessary based on reason, not that it just happens randomly, or that things could be otherwise.

The very smart dog might also draw up a whole system of philosophy for his surroundings in a similar way. And it would all be a huge delusion. Likewise, according to Hume, we don't have ideal forms and pure powers of reason in most applications; we have animal conditioning, experience, and the delusion that we figure things out by pure reason. It is logically *necessary* that if all boxes have corners, and a particular object is a box, that the object has corners. But it is absolutely *not* necessary that a signpost was built by a person, that a flame would burn, or that an oil drop would deflect a certain amount due to a certain amount of charge.[59] Nor is

---

[59] Millikan's Oil Drop Experiment led to the discovery of electrons

it necessary that all bodies would attract each other (gravity). These things are just what we have observed throughout our lifetimes, and none of them that we think of like the dog does ("of course...makes perfect sense") are any more necessary than that food would follow the bell ringing. Logic has nothing to do with such conclusions or expectations, which are based only on experience rather than on true reason.

It's also disheartening to realize that if there is no pure reason, then even the experience and resulting guesses that we do have are not taken and performed by us like the angel-man cognizing that the rational world statistically is this or that. Instead, our experience and guesses and all the rest of our thoughts would be just the work of an organism being impressed on by its senses and adapting for survival. Even a rat learns by experience that a glowing red bar will burn him, but it's not reason by which he figures that out.

So some doubt is cast on the validity of our reasoning abilities by these ideas, but it is easy to show that we do have something more than the animal instinct. Even Hume himself did *not* believe that pure logic doesn't exist, although many have represented him that way. He just believed that reason is limited to particular areas and that we are mistaken if we think we can apply it elsewhere. He recognized that there is a realm where pure logic and necessity exist and work.

Immanuel Kant (German, 1724-1804, and another of the smartest instances of our species) concluded there is such a thing as reason as well, that its use is valid and, further, that it is the highest possible virtue; even higher than natural compassion for others.[60] I

---

[60] Roger Scruton, *German Philosophers: Kant, Hegel, Schopenhauer, and Nietzsche* (Oxford: Oxford University Press, 1997), 82.

do not know of any respected philosopher, in fact, who denies that reason is valid.

Mathematics also demonstrates the validity of the tool. Physicists have experiment, as well as logic for use in their trade, but in mathematics there is no experiment to be done.[61] Mathematicians do not propose something and then go to the lab to observe an electron accelerate, or to watch the path of a particle in order to see if a theory is true. They determine if something is true *solely* by logic.[62] They'll question if a statement is true, and then go and apply the tool within their own brains to find out. The mathematician possesses access inside himself to this tool, as we all do, and he takes a proposition and fires up the chemical analyzer to see what the verdict is. His mind is the laboratory where truth is determined, as it is for all of us when we apply reason. And the accuracy of the tool used in the lab of our mind is demonstrated in the progress that mathematics has made over many years. There are thousands of mathematical statements (theorems) that have been proved — probably several hundred-thousand. It's real and it works.

One example showing this is the Pythagorean Theorem. Below is a proof for it (which anyone can skip that wants to):

---

[61] The physical universe tells physicists what's true and what isn't, and they use logic to interpret what the experimental results mean. For them, physical reality is the factor that determines truth.

[62] Mathematicians do describe having senses of things and having intuition that guides, but those are not proof and provide no agreement or advancement. No mathematician would take the word of another who claimed to "just know" that Fermat's Theorem was true, any more than a person would just take the word of someone who claimed to "just know" that human beings are reincarnated. Only logical argument resolves without a doubt and unanimously.

Begin with the right triangle ABC and draw in the line segment CH, dividing ABC into two other triangles (both right triangles also). Now there are three triangles: ABC, AHC, and BCH. Note that ABC and AHC have the same angle at vertex A. They also have a right angle, which means that the remaining unknown angle of each triangle (θ)

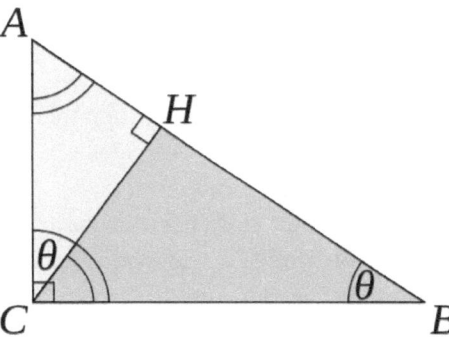

is also the same (the total is 180, always, so the remaining angle of the two must be equal). Because the angles of these two triangles are all the same, the *ratios* of the corresponding sides of the two triangles will also be the same—this means that one triangle is just the other one miniaturized or enlarged. The ratios between the sides are the same, just like the length of your arm compared to the length of your leg would be the same regardless of whether you were shrank/shrunk to a little action figure, or enlarged to a giant. So the number you get by dividing the longest side of the triangle by the shortest side, for example, will be the same for each triangle (AC/AH = BC/CH). The same goes for the other corresponding sides, and all of these similarities also apply with the triangle BCH.

So, ratios of the sides can be written:

BC/AB = BH/BC and AC/AB = AH/AC.

By simple algebra this can be re-written as

$(BC)^2 = (AB)(BH)$ and $(AC)^2 = (AB) \times (AH)$.

So,

$(BC)^2 + (AC)^2 = (AB) \times (BH) + (AB) \times (AH)$.

And just applying a little simplification to the right side of the equation shows that this is

$(AB) \times ((BH)+(AH))$,

and this, of course, is

$$(AB) \times (AB) = (AB)^2.$$

Look back; we just arrived at $(BC)^2 + (AC)^2 = (AB)^2$, which is the Pythagorean Theorem. And I'm sure that this is exciting to everyone. The length of the hypotenuse squared equals the sum of the squares of the other two sides of a right triangle.

Opinion and belief has nothing to do with this theorem or with any other idea in the world of things that answer to logic. Only an irrational person could disagree that the theorem is true. Logic exists and it has discovered truth. I'll also point out that our use of logic is involved in this example and other places even before the proofs are begun. For example, the fact that the amount of "angle" in a triangle must always be the same, is something we know. But how do we know it? We could set up some sticks and measure, but that isn't necessary for us here. If one side gets longer, the angle opposite to it gets larger accordingly, and the other angles get smaller accordingly. We can see that in our minds, and it is not animal instinct or experience that allows us to conclude as we do that, "the amount of 'angle' in any triangle is always equal."[63] Or when we see that the triangles ABC and AHC, or any triangles, have two of the same angles, it is logic that allows us to deduce that the third angle of the two triangles must be equal also. That is necessary. It would not only be bizarre and irrational that they could have two equal angles but that the third would be different, but it would be *impossible*. And how exactly do we know that again? *Logic*: this tool-thing that we can access. Without our access to it, we could never see or know any of this. And whether logic is an ability of the homo sapien like jumping is to frogs, or whether it is like a spiritual

---

[63] In two dimensions. Apparently if a triangle is projected onto a spherical surface, things can vary.

reservoir separate from us that we have some access to, *it works* and it is certain. That is important to recognize.

Conclusion

And the reason it matters that there is such a thing, again, is that, without it, humanity will never be able to determine if there is a God, or to answer any of our other questions with certainty. To repeat also, there is no other way for the species to find answers or make progress the way we have in science. Individuals may become confident of answers, as I became confident, but their personal experience will never convince everyone else, and there will always have to be trust involved, even within that person who had the experience. And, beyond that, even if God did reveal himself to the whole world directly, that event would not convince people who hadn't been born yet. The ones who saw God's revelation could write it down and maintain ceremonies to remember it, and teach it to their kids but, generations later, not everyone would believe that it happened. There have been a whole lot of fairy tales made up over the millennia by our ancestors, and there has been a lot of stuff told to us by older people that was wrong. There's good reason for us to doubt.

To repeat, *the only thing that would answer the questions of God or eternal life, or the other biggest questions permanently, and for the whole race, would be either continual direct revelation from God, or a logical demonstration.* Without one of those things there will never be agreement and there will always be doubts.

It was clear from the proof given of the Pythagorean Theorem, as it is clear from all of math and from a lot of physics, that there is such a thing as pure logic. It is real, and it works. The greatest philosophers agree on this also. So…wonderful. I'm not sure that a starving man or hurting kid or any of the rest of us are going to be helped or comforted by that fact.

It's clear now that logic is a real tool, but what we really want to know is whether there is a God, if he cares about us, and if we will go on existing after death. And, again, the only way those questions could be answered in a conclusive fashion would be either continual revelation from God, or by logic. The first possibility is completely out of our control. And without being able to know the future to begin with, we have no idea whether anything like a possible future revelation from God could ever happen. So we are left asking whether logic can answer these things. And the question becomes, then, what the limits of logic are. Wherever those limits fall, that is our answer to how much the human species can ever know in metaphysics.

Gödel's Theorem

One hint as to what the limits of logic are may come from mathematics, and my discussion would not be complete if I didn't cover this. The question began earlier in this form: "can we ever discover truth in metaphysics as we have in science?" In order to answer that question, we must answer this one: "what limits us in metaphysics?" That question was addressed in the last chapter. And to answer what limits us in metaphysics, we must know what the limits of logic are, since it is the only tool available to us.

This is how investigations go. They start from broader questions to more specific and better aimed ones. The question of "who robbed the bank" might come down to answering the question of whether a specific person stopped at the grocery store Tuesday after work. In our case the broader question of whether the human species could ever learn answers about God and eternal life led to the question of the limits of logic. But this still isn't the end of the trail. Asking that last question is really the same thing as asking "how much can be proved," or whether all questions can be answered with certainty. If a theorem or statement is proved, it is always proved by logic. So, if we know that all things can be proved, we will know that logic could answer everything for us.

This boring and tedious stuff is worth reading because we will never, ever know the answer to any religious question if logic cannot apply to all areas. If we know that *all* questions can be answered with certainty, i.e., by proof, then we know that it's possible to make progress in metaphysics.

Rephrasing the original question in this form is worthwhile because there's a mathematical theorem that might answer it. This chapter gets a little bit technical and anyone uninterested in it could skip to the last paragraph for the conclusion. But, as far as I am aware, applications of this theorem represent the closest that mankind has ever come to answering any religious question. I'll mention also that, since I am no expert in this area and I hadn't held any personal beliefs before reading about the topic, I have presented this chapter in a format with less filtering so that each reader can see more for himself what those people more familiar with the theorem have said.

Kurt Gödel (1906-78) actually proved that there are things in the world of math that can never be proved. His work that demonstrates this is known as the *Incompleteness Theorem* and it is something that might hold promise for helping the human race inch forward a little bit, *for certain*. It would be the first inch we had ever progressed over our thousands of years of trying, so it would be an important one. [64]

Paul Davies describes the theorem to mean that "mathematical statements exist(ed) for which *no* systematic procedure could determine whether they are either true or false."[65] Another expert, Jeff Buechner, says the theorem means that "there are truths of arithmetic that can be expressed within the formal system, but which cannot be proved within it."[66] And that limitation on our ability to prove does not only apply to arithmetic. Buechner goes on to describe that "there is a good deal of mathematical

---

[64] There are actually two theorems, closely linked. The main result is the first one.

[65] Paul Davies, *The Mind of God* (New York: Simon & Schuster, 1992), 100-1.

[66] Jeff Buechner, "Are the Gödel Incompleteness Theorems Limitative Results for the Neurosciences?," *Journal of Biological Physics* 36, no. 1 (2010): 27.

evidence that the phenomenon of incompleteness is pervasive throughout mathematics."[67]

This result overall is remarkable. What it means is that there are things that can never be proved, by anyone...in *mathematics*, where logical proof is the guide and the sole test of truth! As Berlinski said, "it is an absolute commitment to proof that distinguishes the mathematician from mystics, psychologists, great masters of the law, physicists, chemists, biologists, writers, sculptors, moguls, maniacs, indeed, from everyone and everybody else. Proof is the mathematician's coin, the one that he must forever clutch."[68] Math is all about proved theorems. The mathematician Bourbaki even summarizes the field as being the discipline of proof: "From the time of the Greeks, to say 'mathematics' has meant the same as to say 'proof,'" —and proof is all about logic.[69] However, Gödel *proved* that logic is incapable of proving an entire realm of truths! So logic is limited even in its home realm and dominion.

At first glance, then, it seems like the Incompleteness Theorem might allow us to at least prove what we may *not* ever be able to figure out, so that we could at least settle that, and give up on the attempt. It might be disappointing to know what you *can't* ever do, but it is still knowledge, and could be helpful in the end. If a man knows that he will never be able to build a house out of the trees that grow around him because their wood is too weak, he could at least spare himself years of work that would be doomed to failure.

But some people have been much more optimistic about the potential of the Incompleteness Theorem, and they have made respectable attempts to answer several age-old questions by using it. *And that is very exciting.* If any such attempt worked, it would be

---

[67] Buechner, 30.

[68] Berlinski, 107.

[69] Vladimir Uspensky, "Gödel's Incompleteness Theorem," *Theoretical Computer Science* 130, (1994): 243, footnote. (Bourbaki is quoted)

equivalent to Leibniz's *"let us calculate!"* That vision for humanity wouldn't be just a dream anymore!

These attempts have been bold, and some have been carried out by our best minds, but extending the theorem outside of math has turned out not to be so easy. I spent around three-hundred hours reading technical papers on this topic, and I picked up that fact, at least. Buechner is, again, an expert in the area, and he describes that even professionals misconstrue important aspects of the theorem's meaning:

> What eluded Hilary Putnam, philosophers, mathematicians, cognitive scientists, and neuroscientists is that the Gödel theorems show that no one—whether the Gödel theorems apply to them or not—can finitistically prove the consistency of Peano arithmetic with mathematical certainty. They do not show that one cannot prove the consistency of Peano arithmetic with less than mathematical certainty.[70]

This means that a lot of experts—real scholars, and very intelligent ones—have missed the application and meaning of the theorem.[71] Buechner's comment also means that the Incompleteness Theorems don't even say that there are truths that can't be proved in math. The theorems only say that there are truths that can't be proven in math with mathematical certainty. And "mathematical certainty" isn't some greater degree of certainty than we could attain in some other way; it just means a technique used for proof. Buechner says, in fact, that "there are few results in mathematics that are proved with mathematical certainty since few mathematicians

---

[70] Buechner, 33.

[71] The question arises of whether Buechner could be wrong too, if so many other experts have been, but he wrote a book exclusively on the theorem, so if anyone could be trusted, it's probably him, and I've deferred to his analysis several times in the chapter since I am no mathematician.

prove their results in a finitary formal system (such as first-order logic)."[72]

So complication is thrown on the Incompleteness Theorems pretty quickly. And their meaning for all of us in life, if there is one, will be harder to figure out. ...And our enthusiasm wanes. Further evidence that this thing is difficult is the simple fact that an entire book was written about misinterpretations of it; titled *Gödel's Theorem: An Incomplete Guide to its Use and Abuse*. Stewart Shapiro reviewed the book for the journal "Philosophia Mathematica," and describes that its goal was "to discuss some alleged consequences of the incompleteness theorems and, in particular, to debunk thoroughly claims in philosophy, religion, and literary criticism that are supposed to be established, or at least bolstered, by incompleteness."[73]

The theorem can't just be carelessly extended to say something such as that there are truths in life that can never be proved—as myself and many other people would like to say. Shapiro notes, for example, that "the undecidability is limited to statements about the natural numbers." This means that the theorem was intended to apply to a part of math, and *only* to math.[74]

Shapiro went on to describe, for example, one naïve assertion regarding the world's largest religion, that might attempt to use Gödel for support,

> It might indeed be good to have a compelling argument against the thesis that the Bible, properly understood,

---

[72] Buechner, 34.

[73] Stewart Shapiro, review of "Gödel's Theorems: An Incomplete Guide to its Use and Abuse," *Philosophia Mathematica* 14, no. 2 (2006): 1. Written by Franzen Torkel.

[74] I realize that I'm giving quote after quote, which would harm a grade on a paper in school, but I'll continue doing this. I've always valued effective communication of ideas above maintaining appearances and I would rather share the experts' own words on this particular topic than my own so that each person can look at it for himself or herself.

> contains every truth about morality. But the incompleteness theorems have nothing to say about this, unless someone shows how to code statements about morality reliably as statements about natural numbers.[75]

That's where readers are supposed to laugh. It's ridiculous to think that moral statements can be coded as statements about numbers, so anyone trying to say that Gödel's theorem supports this or that theory about the Bible, or any other moral issue, is equally ridiculous.

Shapiro describes a proposition on the other side also that shows the care that has to be taken with applications:

> Suppose, for example, that somebody claims that the Bible is incomplete, and therefore it cannot be the last word—thus invoking Gödel to refute certain fundamentalist themes. If there is a formalization of arithmetic in the Bible, and if the consequent relation we are to use in drawing consequences from the Bible is recursively enumerable, then there will indeed be truths of arithmetic that are not decided by scripture.[76]

That is supposed to be another laugh because there really is not much formalized arithmetic in the Bible. Again, extending Gödel's theorems to any part of life is not so easily done, or it may not even be possible at all.

But not everyone who has tried to use the theorems to support arguments in metaphysics handles them inexpertly. In the expert's own words:

---

[75] Shapiro, 263-4.

[76] Shapiro, 263.

> Some alleged applications and consequences of incompleteness cannot be dismissed as easily as this. The Lucas-Penrose thesis (or theses) do not seem to turn on such elementary misunderstandings of what the incompleteness theorems say. Lucas and Penrose themselves certainly understand the mathematics.[77]

Smart people, including J.R. Lucas mentioned above, have tried to use the theorems to prove, for example, that the mind is not just matter—that it's more than just various arrangements and movements of the cells in our brains. They've tried to solve that age old argument conclusively using Gödel's theorem. Incredible!

Lucas voices his belief on this attempt: "Gödel's theorem seems to me to prove that Mechanism is false, that is, that minds cannot be explained as machines."[78] This is a very, very big deal and is not pertinent only to the world of books. As Jaroslav Peregrin says: "Far from being of interest only for narrow specialists, this interpretation ascribes to Gödel's result the power of deciding one of the most irritating conundrums mankind has ever considered: namely *can there be a mechanical mind?*"[79] Again, metaphysics is not just the hobby of some nerds. The questions, answers, and attempts at answers, matter to everyone, and if we have ever hoped for any scientific endeavor to be successful in all of our centuries here, we should hope for this one. If our minds are not simply physical, it would mean that there is such a thing as spirit; that there is more to this world. Actually proving such a thing would change the world.

To put this in perspective again, the Incompleteness Theorem is the only respectable effort I know of to settle for good any of the questions we want to know in our lost world floating

---

[77] Shapiro, 264.

[78] Jaroslav Peregrin, "Gödel, Truth & Proof," *Journal of Physics: Conference Series* 82 (2007): 3.

[79] Peregrin, 3.

through space. Essentially everything else I've seen is simply fodder for endless and inconclusive arguments extended through thousands of pages of words. But it is amazing that an attempt using real logic could be made to prove an answer to any of the issues that have plagued us for so long. *"Let us calculate."* That has never happened elsewhere in human history as far as I know. Here, with The Incompleteness Theorem, though, an answer was tried at one of our questions in a way that would leave no doubt remaining!

...*But these attempts have been disproved.* And there it is; any hope that there might have been is disappointed. Buechner concludes that "no finitary human being can use the Gödel incompleteness theorems to show there are proof-theoretic powers human cognition has that no computational device intended to simulate it can capture."[80] I.e., no one can use the theorem to prove that we are not machines, that we are not simply organisms, that there is something spiritual to us. Buechner and others support that conclusion convincingly and leave little room for doubt.

In the end, generally, and unfortunately, it really doesn't look like the theorem will be able to answer anything in the positive. But the less ambitious attempt involving the theorem should be considered again, which is whether it might tell us anything about what we *can't* know in life. If it can tell us what questions we can't answer, ever, period, we will at least know that. If a person is sick, it is at least some comfort to know what the problem is, even if nothing can be done about it, rather than for it to remain some unknown killer.

As it turns out, though, we probably can't use the theorems to tell us for certain what we can't know either. The mathematician Alonzo Church actually proved that it's impossible to tell which statements are unprovable in mathematics. So even if the theorems could be applied to life in general, which is itself in doubt, they still

---

[80] Buechner, 34.

Gödel's Theorem   133

could not inform us of whether answering our questions for certain was possible or not.[81]

Peregrin dismisses attempts to extend the theorems to metaphysics and even discludes the possibility that they can be extended to most branches of mathematics. In one of his papers he works through what the theorem really says and how it is formulated mathematically, then he spends the rest of the time proposing *accurate* interpretations for what it means. His interpretation and final word is this:

> I think that this exegetical exercise indicates that we should be wary of seeing Gödel's result as bringing about a simple moral. Gödel's proof is a piece of mathematics (a masterpiece, for that matter!), whose significance surely *does* outrun the boundaries of mathematics; but does not do so in a way which would be transparent and which could be identified without a deep understanding of the matter.[82]

Peregrin does not exactly imply that this is an understanding that even he does not possess, but he makes it clear that he does not know how the theorem could be applied beyond mathematics, assuming that is even possible. He did know enough, though, to accurately discredit all previous attempts to do so.

What this all means, basically, is that the Incompleteness Theorem certainly has not helped the human race figure out anything about life and knowledge and that we are as much in the dark as we ever were. The theorem does not even provide us with certainty that there are things we *can't* ever know for certain. It's like a situation where the universe keeps allowing a guy to spend all of his money and effort year after year trying to build his dream, when it simply cannot work, instead of the man being able to find out that

---

[81] Although, I think a glance at history shows that none of them can be proved.

[82] Peregrin, 8.

it's impossible and being able to give up at long last. About the only help or comfort the theorems may give us would be to convince more people that some things do go beyond the realm of logic.

So, interminable uncertainty strikes again and the question of mind as machine and all the other questions are out of the hands of our very smartest people and away from rigorous attempts at achieving real answers, and are back into the hands of any slob that wants to guess at them. As Kant said, in metaphysics "Everybody, who with respect to all other sciences observes a wary silence, speaks masterfully, and boldly passes judgment in questions of metaphysics, because here to be sure their ignorance does not stand out clearly in relation to the science of others"[83] and in metaphysics, "anyone, usually ignorant in all other things, lays claim to a decisive opinion, since in this region there are in fact still no reliable weights and measures with which to distinguish profundity from shallow babble."[84] The Incompleteness Theorem almost changed this so that profundity—and not only profound statements, but *true* statements—could be distinguished from the endless babble. It *almost* made it so that the very smartest people could figure out if there is a God or if we have a soul—as they figured out that the planets' orbits are elliptical and that Fermat's theorem is true—and then share the answers with everyone. But not quite.

---

[83] Kant, *Prolegomena*, 14.

[84] Kant, *Prolegomena*, 6.

The Limits of Reason

A couple chapters back I asked what limits us in metaphysics, and concluded that it was the limit of logic, since that is the only tool available to us to make progress in metaphysics. Now we will look directly at what the limits of logic actually are.

The Greeks were basically the first group of people to use the standard-issue *brain*® to figure things out, and this may be the biggest reason for their lasting fame. One author has said that if it hadn't been for the plague in Athens during the Peloponnesian War, man might have landed on the moon in 69 instead of 1969. The Greeks were the first to apply actual thinking (logic and argument) to either science or metaphysics, and the way that their efforts went is representative of the way the human species' efforts have always gone. What limited them is what limits us all, but philosophical discussions back then seemed simpler than they are now, so looking at a couple examples of their thought is a straightforward way to see how our efforts go.

Heracleitus was a pre-Socratic philosopher (~535-475 BC) living before the Greeks really got warmed up to explain and discover. And he said, "This *cosmos* none of the gods nor human beings made, but it always was and is and will be an everliving fire, being lit in measures and extinguished in measures."[85] While this is beautiful and poignant, there is no argument to support it, and

---

[85] Heracleitus, fr. 30. (24)

Heracleitus probably never gave any explanation for how he claimed to know it. So it would have to go into the category of bald conjecture. And bald conjecture is all that most cultures have ever given: the world being perched on the back of a great turtle, particular bits of land being drops off the sword of some great god thing, the sun being a god, certain animals being gods, etc., with no argument for support. Heracleitus's statement was not so unlikely, but since there was no logical support attempted for it, it goes into that pile as well.

Later on in Greece, though, philosophers usually made some effort to argue their points.[86] (And it was no coincidence that most of them no longer believed in horse gods or the value of sacrificing people to the sun.) Sextus Empiricus gives one example of an early philosophical argument: "If Zeus is a god," he says, "Posidon too, being his brother, will be a god. But if Posidon is a god, the [river] Achelous too will be a god. And if the Achelous is, so is the Nile. If the Nile is, so are all rivers. If all rivers are, streams too would be gods. If streams were, torrents would be. But streams are not. Therefore Zeus is not a god either....Therefore there are no gods." And he says, "If the sun is a god, day too would be a god (for day is nothing but the sun above the earth)"[87] etc. But days aren't gods, so the sun isn't a god, so there are no gods. This is a good representative example of an attempt to apply reason to metaphysics—to the questions we wonder about and want to know the most—and the concept is momentous. *It was an attempt to apply our one irrefutable tool to religion.*

Thanks to logic, the Greeks also knew, for hundreds of years before Christ, that the earth was round. One proof of this was in the way shadows were cast by sticks in the ground. Another was that they could observe ships becoming visible over the horizon. "If the

---

[86] And argument always appeals to logic.

[87] Sextus Empiricus, *Against the Professors*, 9.139-41. (388).

earth was flat and a ship was approaching in the distance, it would not become visible suddenly; therefore..." Logic works.

Or, Plato and all of the group he was a part of believed that there is a single creator which they called "The One" that explains everything and is self-existent. They also believed in "The Intellect" which is united with the One, and they believed that souls come from there. Whether or not this is true, it's not as dumb as what people were believing before. So, thought, guided by reason, for the first time, was having its effect and seemed to be furthering the human race.

Brains were being applied and the arguments were worth something, but it became obvious pretty quickly that what worked in other places (science) just didn't seem to be working in religion beyond a very simple level, and we lurched to a halt about as soon as we had begun. Sextus's argument was not empty, for example, because, if the sun was a god, who could say that the day would not also logically have to be a god? It is not clearly an incorrect conclusion, but whatever *is* true, he didn't show it, and no one would mistake his argument for proof. Add it to the hundred-mile-high pile of guesswork.

And it's discouraging that an argument so simple as Sextus's can't be proved true or untrue. Like the *Discover* article on the proof for stacked cannonballs that the professors couldn't decide on, no one could really decide on this one about the gods, or on others like Anselm's supposed proof for God's existence. In the mathematical area, logic got us a long way and it continues to take us farther and farther even after thousands of years of traveling. In *metaphysics* logic got us a little way so that we don't think rivers and planets are gods anymore, but its usefulness in this area hit insurmountable problems almost right away. The mathematical issues with the cannonballs were very complicated, so it seems fair that we would have problems there, but Anselm's proof and Sextus's argument are incredibly simple and it seems like they could and should be able to be resolved by anyone. But they never have been.

That is how attempts to answer religious questions *always* end up, and I don't see that much has changed in the intervening millennia. Modern philosophers are able to write much more complex arguments, and they don't make such sweeping assumptions as the earlier men did, but until there are newspaper headlines describing a breakthrough where someone has actually proved something—even the idea of which, again, we've learned to laugh at—we can remain pretty sure that they've had no more success than Socrates did, and that the human species' perfect record of zero-for-a-billion has been maintained.

And that is discouraging because the conclusion from earlier was that the only way we will ever answer our religious questions with certainty is by logic. It is our only tool and our only ship. We will go only as far as it can take us.

But what about the future?

So we have failed in the past. But what about the future? What are the limits of logic? Could we succeed? There is one principle related to this question that is worth mentioning: Just because something hasn't happened yet, doesn't mean that it cannot happen. Something that mathematicians did involving Fermat's Last Theorem is a good example of this. Before the theorem was proved to be true, mathematicians had set up computers to run through all the possible numbers to see if they could find any set that would prove the theorem to be false. If that happened, no one would have to spend their time trying to prove it. The computers ran for years. But the thing is that they could have run for a million more years and, no matter how many sets of numbers they could have tried, it would never prove that one day they might not find a set of numbers that *did* solve the equation.

This is to say that experience can never prove that something *isn't* possible. Only the power of the mind can do that; by our use of logic. So, none of humanity's experience in the past, or our past failures could prove that we won't one day be able to solve our questions, and the question remains: Could logic ever allow us to answer the biggest questions of this existence? Our best hope for proving an answer to this lies in the efforts of our most brilliant minds. What have they said about our chances for the future?

Locke's answer

One of the first people to question how far logic could go was John Locke (1632-1704).[88] Will Durant says that with Locke's *Essay Concerning Human Understanding*, "reason, for the first time in modern thought, had turned in upon itself, and philosophy had begun to scrutinize the instrument which it so long had trusted."[89] David Snyder comments that Locke's *Essay* "can be viewed at least in part as an attempt to make room for true faith by establishing the limits of reason and certainty."[90, 91]

It was as if we'd been drilling for years at a wall that separates us from answers to our religious questions, and that we'd tried one thing and another, but finally a materials scientist took a look, put a calm hand on our shoulder as we were hunched over the jackhammer, and said that we should examine the properties of the

---

[88] The skeptics in ancient times doubted that any knowledge was possible but they do not seem to have ever analyzed logic itself and its limits at length.

[89] Will Durant, *The Story of Philosophy* (New York: Pocket Books, 1953), 256.

[90] David Snyder, "Faith and Reason in Locke's Essay," *Journal of the History of Ideas* 47, no. 2 (April 1986): 197.

[91] Thomas Aquinas, though, may have been the first to distinguish between topics that could be known by reason, and those that could not be known by reason. Locke's views on the separation of worlds of reason and faith were similar (Faith and Reason, 200).

tools we were using, like the bit hardness, and the chemical composition of the wall, and see if it was theoretically possible to make any progress in the first place.

Locke's definition for *reason* seems to have been different from all those given by people before him. He said that it is "a faculty in man, that faculty whereby man is supposed to be distinguished from beasts, and wherein it is evident he much surpasses them."[92] So it's a faculty or a tool. And how far can this faculty take us? Can it be used to prove that there is a God or a soul, as we have tried to do? Locke said that it could not. He and Thomas Aquinas were the first to conclude that there are particular areas that reason can be applied and a set of propositions it can be used to discover and demonstrate, and *another* area and set of propositions that it cannot demonstrate. This other set of propositions is the realm of faith, not reason, they said.

Locke describes that we can have no knowledge of things that are beyond the experience we could possibly have using our natural faculties. Those questions are "above reason" and "when revealed, [are] *the proper matter of faith.*"[93] We can't discover religious ideas physically (they're beyond any experience we can have by the use of our physical senses), so only revelation can show them to us. And when that revelation happens, "faith" is the response, not knowledge. As Locke said, for example: "Thus, [the idea] that part of the angels rebelled against God, and thereby lost their first happy state: and that the dead shall rise, and live again: these and the like, being beyond the discovery of reason, are purely matters of faith, with which reason has directly nothing to do."[94] We believe things like those, or any other abstract things like them, by using faith, not reason.

---

[92] John Locke, *An Essay Concerning Human Understanding* (1690), IV, xvii, 1. (113).

[93] Locke, IV, xviii, 7. (p 123)

[94] Locke, IV, xviii, 7.

So there's the conclusion of one very intelligent and thoughtful man: "*no; reason cannot solve everything."* And this means that we should give up on the metaphysics because we will never have answers to our questions.[95] Of course, though, Locke couldn't prove this any more than Plato could prove that there is a soul.

Hume's answer

One of the other most intelligent human beings to have ever addressed this issue was Hume. He basically agreed with Locke, and his analysis is more lucid and complete than any other that I've seen. His entire approach to philosophy was centered on the human being and what we are capable of—what our powers of thought are. Instead of just setting a course for the next galaxy over, like essentially everyone else had always done for centuries, he thought it would be wise to look down first and examine what kind of ship the human race was riding in. He determined that this turns out to be something like a propeller plane that will never, *ever* get us beyond a certain point. Hume says, as one example, that when we go trying to figure out whether God made a universe that can run on its own, and creatures capable of free action, or whether God determines every single event, our minds have led us

> quite beyond the reach of our faculties, when it leads to conclusions so extraordinary, and so remote from common life and experience. We are got into fairy land, long ere we have reached the last steps of our theory; and *there* we have no reason to trust our common methods of argument, or to think that our usual analogies and probabilities have any

---

[95] Locke said we *could* know certainly that there is a God, by reason. He even gives an example of an argument for it—something like, that since we exist as beings, there must be an omnipotent creator. The argument does have merit, like the others; but that someone as smart as him could consider that argument or any other as being *certainty* is very surprising. If there was a logical proof of God's existence, the world would be a different kind of place.

authority. Our line is too short to fathom such immense abysses.[96]

Likewise, our limited tools could never allow us to determine logically whether there *is* a God or an afterlife, or to let us answer any other question that is not within our experience.

Hume concluded that the limits and proper realm of our vessel—the good ship, *The Logic*—are "quantity and number, and that all attempts to extend this more perfect species of knowledge beyond these bounds are mere sophistry and illusion."[97] Reason, or, as he called it, "knowledge and demonstration," is that "more perfect species of knowledge" because things discovered by this tool result in *certainty* when the tool has been used properly.

So, according to Hume there *is* certainty, but only when logic is applied correctly. This seems obvious. Compare the proof of the Pythagorean Theorem to Plato's argument for the immortality of the soul, for example, and there is clearly a big difference (who knows exactly *why* there is, but the difference is there). One of those two is truly certain and can be demonstrated, while the other is not even close. The comparison of any genuine logical proof to any other form of knowledge we have in life in general shows a distinct difference also. For example, we know that most of the first colonists in American were English and we know that the people around us today are, or are not, trustworthy. But knowledge of things like these depends on entirely different methods than logical proof, and they can come into doubt much more easily.

We weren't there to see colonial America, for example, and, as a lot of people have recognized, the historical record isn't always accurate. We have also certainly all been wrong in our judgments about people around us. Again, things like these are not determined

---

[96] Hume, section VII, part I. (358).

[97] Hume, section XII, part III. (428).

by logic and there is no necessity about them. Logical proofs, though, can be demonstrated at any time and they are necessarily true. Issues determined this way are definitely a "more perfect species of knowledge." They are truly certain.

Hume says that in all the other areas of life outside mathematics or physics, which he calls "matters of fact," things,

> are not ascertained in the same manner...The contrary of every matter of fact is still possible; because it can never imply a contradiction, and is still conceived by the mind with the same facility and distinctness...*that the sun will not rise tomorrow* is no less intelligible a proposition, and implies no more contradiction than the affirmation, *that it will rise*.[98]

It's easy to see that he is right. (And, to repeat, what this is about is the limit of logic, which I concluded earlier also determines the limit of what mankind can *ever* be able to learn about religion. This is Hume's answer to that question.) There is no *necessity* about there being a soul or that there is continued existence after death. We can easily conceive that we might *not* have a soul or that when we die we cease to exist. But we *cannot* easily conceive that one moving object that's ahead of another and going faster than the other could ever be passed by it. *That* is impossible. Or the amount of angle in a triangle must always be the same, and we cannot conceive anything different. [99] All issues that are truly determined logically are the same—there is necessity that they would be one way and no other.

Hume's conclusion is similar to a somewhat enigmatic statement of Parmenides from way, way back. "The only two ways of inquiry in thought: The one, that it is and that it is impossible that 'not-to-be' is; The other that it is not and that it is necessary that 'not-

---

[98] Hume, section IV, part I.   322-23

[99] Again, in two dimensions supposedly.

to-be' is, Is the way of Conviction (for she accompanies Truth)," meaning, I think, that the only way that thought results in certainty is if necessity is involved. Logic only applies if the conclusions could not possibly be otherwise—"it is and that it is impossible that 'not-to-be' is." For another example, that the sum of two positive numbers could be less than either one separately is impossible; impossible that this "not-to-be" could be.

So there is a way of thought resulting in real certainty, but it definitely doesn't apply to religion.[100] There is obviously a chasm between "the science of quantity and number" and religious or strictly factual issues which have no necessity involved. Only one of these realms allows our tool of logic to be successfully applied to it, and one of them is certain in a way which the other never will be. Hume says that human understanding is "by no means fitted for such remote and abstruse subjects" as religion and metaphysics.[101] According to him we should not think that we can prove or settle any of life's questions—unless mathematical topics are considered to be part of life's questions.

Personally, I am really not interested in reading more theories and arguments on why God must or must not exist, what the soul is, the meaning of language, or any others. But I do enjoy reading philosophies about life and happiness. And that is the realm Hume describes to be philosophy's "true and proper province."[102] Like Locke, Hume was not optimistic about our ability to ever make progress in metaphysics as we have in science.

---

[100] Parmenides, I.53, fr. 2.   32

[101] Hume, section I.   312

[102] Hume, section VIII, part II.

Kant's answer

Another of the other smartest human beings that has ever applied his mind to these things was Immanuel Kant. And I should point out here, maybe—since my writing may be getting tedious for some people at this point—that I describe the findings of men like these in a little bit of detail because they are the closest equivalents there have been in metaphysics to the geniuses that have triumphed in science. Our heroes that have jumped the great hurdles in math, physics, and medicine were our smartest people, and it was *brains* that enabled them to do it—brains that could wield our one unequivocal tool better than all other people. The equivalent brains in metaphysics have been men like Kant, and they have tried to use the same avenue as the scientists to find answers. If anyone could leap the hurdles to answer our questions in life definitively, it would be guys like Locke, Hume, and Kant who were extremely intelligent and who dedicated their life and energy to trying. This is why their conclusions are worth sharing in my attempt to describe what answers might exist to cure humanity's uncertainty in this world.

So, Kant agreed with Hume that logic is a valid tool and that it belongs to the domain of experience and that it can be taken no further. And, like Hume, instead of just launching off into hundreds of pages more worth of guesses and flawed arguments like previous philosophers, he first asked if metaphysics was even possible—i.e., if it would even be possible for us to answer any of our questions to begin with. [103] These two thinkers focused on *us* and what our capabilities actually are and what they can do. Can the drill bit cut the wall to begin with? And let's take a look at what kind of vessel we're in before we set out.

Kant thought that all human beings possess "categories" such as length and space, through which we interpret sensation, so that our physical sensations are not just incoherent jigglings of

---

[103] Metaphysics, or equivalently in his words, "synthetic a priori knowledge."

atoms, but are put together into coherent experience. Logic or reason is then applied to our experience to make sense of it in turn. His "categories" are the elements of our thought without which we would be like a computer without any programs to run. They are all of our abilities of thought: concepts like space, time, length, greatness, cause, etc. We truly do seem to have been born with these things, and without them we could not function.

These categories or concepts are similar to Plato's forms, which are like pure ideas or concepts. Plato did not consider the forms to be tools so much as Kant considered his categories to be, but Plato did see them as necessary for any kind of thought. In *Parmenides*, for example, Plato has his character Parmenides say to Socrates "if a man, fixing his attention on these and the like difficulties, does away with ideas of things and will not admit that every individual thing has its own determinate idea which is always one and the same, he will have nothing on which his mind can rest; and so he will utterly destroy the power of reasoning, as you seem to me to have particularly noted."[104] Without the forms or ideas, we would be in a straight-jacket, or we would truly be 100% animals with no self-awareness, like my friend Lae.

Similarly, another genius-level philosopher—Whewell—said that humans have "Ideas" that are like Kant's categories: "These Fundamental Ideas are conditions without which the external world can neither be observed nor conceived"[105] Will Durant indicates that there is even something close to agreement on this issue, saying that Kant settled "once for all, that the external world is known to us only as sensation; and that the mind is no mere helpless *tabula rasa*, the inactive victim of sensation, but a positive agent, selecting and

---

[104] Plato, *Parmenides*, p 378-79.

[105] Steffen Ducheyne, "Kant and Whewell on Bridging Principles between Metaphysics and Science," *Kant-Studien* 102, no. 1 (March, 2011): 41.

reconstructing experience as experience arrives."[106] I don't believe that anything is ever settled, but Kant came close to a conclusive result on this topic. It is generally agreed that we have a certain set of capabilities of thought. But the important question is how far these ideas/forms/categories/capabilities of thought can take us and where they can be applied.

Kant had an answer to that question, but his writing is notoriously difficult and obscure, and it's probably best to look at expert analysis of his thought rather than his own words; which I have done here. He said that applying these "categories" or concepts to things that we have no experience of is misusing them, like trying to use a word processor to do artwork. He said that "concepts divorced from their 'empirical conditions' are empty." Trying to apply these tools, like logic, to things that are outside the realm of experience is hopeless because, without something concrete to operate on (experience,) they are empty. Kant says that these mental tools, which are the only ones that we have, "can *never* admit of *transcendental* but *always* only of *empirical* employment," i.e., the human programs can only operate on empirical things (things that we can experience). [107] We cannot experience the beginning of the universe or run an experiment to determine where the afterlife is, so our abilities of thought, or our programs, can't operate on those things in order to find answers to them. According to Kant, attempting to apply "pure reason" to figure out if we have a soul, or to figure out any of those other religious questions is a hopeless pursuit.

---

[106] Durant, 287.

[107] Roger Scruton, *German Philosophers* (Oxford: Oxford University Press: 1997), 47.

The answer of modern philosophers

Other philosophers have addressed the issue in more modern times also, and it doesn't look like anything has changed since Heraclitus. Talking about our attempts to apply the methods that succeed in the sciences (i.e. logic) to religious or metaphysical questions, Paul Horwich of New York University says

> It is far from obvious that they [our scientific methods of applied logic] should (or even can) be extended to philosophy—which is clearly not just one more empirical science....we find ourselves with so-called "intuitions"—which are notoriously variable....Obviously, what we have here is only a pale shadow of the scientific method—a distorted and watered-down variant of it. One unsurprising upshot—both in ethics and other domains of philosophy—is a striking paucity of definite results. Cases in which particular systematic theories emerge as objectively "the best" are few and far between.[108]

So there is agreement between the set of philosophers discussed here that reason cannot solve every question, and that we are basically foolish to try to answer religious questions through logic. But others still think that it can work, as they demonstrate, since they're still trying to do it. In general there is no agreement on this, or on anything else.

For example, Kant is usually thought to be the greatest modern philosopher, or at least the most influential, so we could possibly take him to be our representative for the smartest of all the human animals. But what was he able to answer for us? That we aren't blank slates and that we have ideas that organize experience. Is that all? This is really not going to help anyone, and even on this

---

[108] Paul Horwich, "Williamson's Philosophy of Philosophy," *Philosophy and Phenomenological Research* 82, no. 2 (March 2011): 525-26

point there isn't consensus that he was right anyway because he couldn't *prove* it; he could only argue for it. I've done enough math to recognize the difference between argument and proof, I've read his argument, and it's not the latter.

I expect there are plenty of philosophers who still disagree with everything Kant ever said. Actually, it's clear from Paul Horwich's introspective paper "Williamson's *Philosophy of Philosophy*" that this is exactly the case. There isn't agreement on Kant's stuff either, and it still hasn't been agreed on that the scientific method *can't* be applied to philosophy to solve everything after all. *So there's uncertainty of the uncertainty!* It's like we tried to move backwards by saying that we can't possibly move forward, so that at least we could move somewhere, but we ended up not even being able to move backwards with a consensus.

Kant was at least correct, though, about the historical condition of knowledge and the performance of reason in metaphysics and religion: "It has not gone so well for human reason in this case. One can point to no single book, as for instance one presents a *Euclid*, and say: this is metaphysics, here you will find the highest aim of this science, knowledge of a supreme being and a future life, proven from principles of pure reason."[109] At least no one could argue with that statement. There *are* no philosophy textbooks describing what is *true*. There are only textbooks describing what one guy said and what another guy said. And it remains this way after the attempts of even our greatest minds.

Ted Warfield sums up the whole thing regarding progress for our species and consensus on religious answers pretty well:

> There are so many different and incompatible answers posed to philosophical questions by even really intelligent philosophers that we can deduce that most philosophers,

---

[109] Kant, *Prolegomena*, 4:271.   24.

> even most intelligent philosophers, have false beliefs about the correct answers to any interesting philosophical question…. I know that because I know that, at least typically, most philosophical views are minority opinions. Each positive philosophical view is usually such that most philosophers think that it is false, and there is typically nothing approaching a consensus on the correct alternative. I can, therefore, infer that most philosophical views are false.[110]

There is no agreement about what's true, and even those who might have happened on the truth would not *know* that they've happened on it.

Conclusion

The reason for going through all of this in the last several chapters has been to look at whether there is a way we can ever be certain of things that the human race desperately wants to know. Uncertainty permeates our lives and is responsible for a lot of our pain. If it didn't, and wasn't, and if we were like buffalo and didn't care about it anyway, I wouldn't waste my time with any of this. But, because of what we are, and because of the pain that uncertainty causes us, this stuff *does* matter, and it's worth knowing as much as possible about the issue. The discomfort we feel from our uncertainty doesn't only apply to the cosmic questions of God and soul and ethics either, but it applies to daily life as well. There aren't going to be any systematic methods for solving those daily battles, but our terror of death and our pain in life from the prospect that there might *not* be a God who cares about us, or a purpose for anything, *could* be answered if someone could prove an answer.

---

[110] Ted Warfield, *Disagreement* (Oxford: Oxford University Press, 2010), 108-9.

And, proving answers doesn't seem at first, or even second glance like it should be outside the realm of possibility.

If our questions could be answered for sure, like questions in science and mathematics have been for so long, we would really be getting somewhere. But it should be clear after this discussion over the last many pages that we *aren't* getting somewhere. I don't know of any "religious" question that philosophy, science, or any other method of thought, whatever it may be called, has answered for us since the dawn of time. Endeavors to find out, based on logic, have shown that the planets are not gods and that there is not a giant turtle holding up the earth, but those and all of the other things we have learned have been matters subject to physical verification. Every single transcendental question we had at the start, we still have now.

There are no textbooks describing our findings in metaphysics or religion because *there are no findings*. And there haven't been any headlines detailing a new discovery, or an award given out for major advancements in metaphysics, because *there have been no advancements*. Nothing is agreed on and no questions have been answered. Our tool of logic has not worked.

But what about the future? And "look at how far we've come!" Well, yes, look at how far we've come in *science;* in empirically verifiable things. A genius might come along in the world of science or math and make real advancements and discoveries that have never been made before and add a lot to our knowledge of the physical universe. He may have the intelligence to jump over that bar that others couldn't. He might be able to see unanswered mathematical truths clearly, or might invent a way to travel faster than the speed of light. But I do not believe that a genius will ever come along and prove, at last, whether there is a God, if we have a soul, or finally answer any of those other questions. Unfortunately. Our beleaguered race will never have a hero of that type. In fact, it's much more likely that a prodigy who gets into these issues will be pretty dumb in the area of real life, whereas he was smart in other areas. Most of us have known individuals just like that, and a disproportionately large number of the legends in math and science throughout history have shown that exact kind of dichotomy—real smart in science; real stupid in life. But even if a genius in *all* things and the best of all humans arrived here, it's not likely that he would be solving any of our religious questions. We've had several thousand years at it now and have proved nothing, so the odds don't look good for the future either.

There's a good illustration of that conclusion from a Tiny Toons® cartoon I saw years ago where one of the bunnies was chained to an alien rocket that was coming to blow up the earth. The situation didn't look good at all and the control room on earth, full of extremely smart guys, didn't know what to do. So they pushed an emergency button, a secret door opened, and a guy with a huge head containing a brain twice the size of anyone else's rolled out. *He* would figure it out. But the alpha-genius analyzed the situation, zipped back into his secret room, and shot off in an escape pod to leave earth. (Not a good sign.) The very smartest realized the attempt was hopeless and he knew better than to try. Maybe the very smartest in the real world would also realize that attempts to *prove* anything or to attain logical certainty of any metaphysical issue is useless.

Based on millennia of experience, it doesn't look like we will figure anything out in religion as we have so many times in science. No supremely gifted individual or society or government task force or machine we can build will ever figure it out. I personally think that it is probably truly impossible. And that is "impossible" not to mean *unlikely*, or extremely unlikely—like it's extremely unlikely that there will ever be a guy the size of a lineman that can play cornerback—but it's impossible in a rigorous and formal sense, i.e., to mean *not possible, ever, period*.

By age twenty-five, before reading any of these things that I've quoted, and before reading a word elsewhere on the topic, I had arrived at these simple conclusions and had realized that a failure to be certain is not an issue of just not trying, or of refusing to believe, but that it's part of our inherent condition. I spent a lot of time doing research to find out what other people have said, not expecting answers, but in order to be able to write something properly researched. I could be criticized for only looking at a few philosophers, but I would hold to what I've concluded regardless of what others have said. When I see newspaper headlines heralding a philosopher's breakthrough, and when I can look over some kind of proof, then I'll change my views on certainty.

None of this is to say that I wouldn't *like* to know. I don't do well trusting, as many people do not. Our species overall has an inability to believe things that can't be touched with our hands or seen with our eyes, or proved by reason, and it is unpleasant for us to have to wonder. But we will never know in this world; not in the way that we know we are sitting on a chair, that matter is made of atoms, or that parallel lines do not cross. If we are going to believe things, we will either have to make a gamble and trust, or we'll have to attain knowledge through some other means, as long as the world remains as it is now—with God in heaven and the human species dwelling down here on the earth.

All this I tested by wisdom and I said, 'I am determined to be wise'—but this was beyond me. Whatever wisdom may be, it is far off and most profound—who can discover it?
(Eccl. 7:23-24)

The Other Way

We aren't sure of religious answers in this world through reason or logic, and the best philosophers agree that we never will be. The race as a whole will never know. But as individuals we *are* capable of some kind of knowledge in these areas, and this is thanks to the part of us that's alive. Logic does not comprehend meaning and it is not capable of feeling, certainty, or doubt. But there is another avenue of knowledge that enables us both to know and understand, even though it is a different type of knowledge than we normally think of. Humanity's desire to find answers is hopeless in one aspect, but it is not hopeless in another.

Sometimes people have the ability to know things which neither they nor anyone else could ever put into words. Even an attempt to verbally explain some of those ideas or feelings is taboo in many parts of society, because explanations just don't seem to work. There is a lot of superstition in some places, and there's uncertainty in every place, but a kind of knowledge that defies explanation can also exist in the same places. Sometimes we can see a little bit, although what we catch glimpses of might only be able to be described with indirect references, like in art.

There are degrees of this abstract type of knowledge as well; not only complete knowledge or complete ignorance. And at the very top of our range—as close as we can get to genuinely grasping things—there's an experience that could never be missed if it happens and could never be forgotten afterwards. It's like having a veil lifted back off of our minds and spirit that had been in place every second of our lives without us even knowing it.

If this experience has happened to someone they have known an inexplicable feeling and perspective that goes way beyond the reaches of reason, and makes their jaw drop and look around wide-eyed at the life they had been living in for so long, bored and blind, without seeing or feeling. During those few and brief moments when it has happened to me I have realized not only that I've been blind all the days of my life and for every moment leading up to it, but also that I'll probably plunge right back into darkness and plod along in a haze again soon after. And, more than that, I grasp that I will also hardly even remember the realization I had where my head got above the clouds for just an instant so that I could see.

We are almost always in a much less clear state in life, though. Animals live in the physical world, and non-physical or non-logical things don't compute with sheep or gazelles, cows, rabbits, gophers, or humans. That is us. The world of food and dirt and cold is usually all we can see. But it appears that we do have a spiritual nature as well, and on some rare occasions it seems to come to life. We *can* feel, understand, and know, but those capacities seem to only come together once in a long while, and not when we choose to make them.

One of these events that I will always remember happened when I was nineteen and was home from school on a break in the fall. I fell asleep one afternoon at around four o'clock in my room in the basement. I almost never sleep during the day, and I had not planned to this time—throughout the course of a year it might happen once. My father and brother came down to the basement and woke me up at about seven, after it was dark, saying they were going somewhere. The instant I woke up I saw this place that we live in with something close to *proper* vision, more clearly than I ever had.[111] It was like coming back to this particular existence after having been in some other place where there wasn't even a memory of this life. The feeling and understanding I experienced with that return was overwhelming and I said out loud, *"life is crazy,"* like a declaration of truth that had to be voiced, whether anyone was there to hear it or not. And my overwhelming feeling and insight was exactly that; that life and this place we're in is crazy. I know that many of us regularly conclude that very same thing that I felt, and the idea has been in catchy refrains in pop songs that teenage girls sing. But we really have no idea, and I saw it in a way like the theoretical *sane* visitor from a sane world would if he took a look at this place that we live in. I think that both my father and brother were affected when they heard my verdict. Maybe they got a sense also that something had happened.

    The main point, though, is that this was something like genuine understanding. I possessed it for about thirty seconds that day, it was on a distinctly separate and higher level than my normal experience, and it seemed to have had nothing at all to do with any effort of mine. The wind comes and goes as it pleases.

    Another occurrence was on a day towards the end of the summer when I was twenty. Again it happened just as I woke up from a rare instance of sleeping during the day. A roommate down the hall was playing a particular song that's still haunting and powerful to me, and I can barely hint at the feeling that came over me. Maybe that life is profound and weighty, and that what we do matters. I was amazed this time as well, largely because I realized how dead I had been every day of my life before then. This later experience was less specific than the previous one, and may have been mostly due to the music, but it was also unforgettable and on a distinctly higher plane than my normal condition. But then, afterwards, it was back down into the shadows where we live every day and do not feel or see.

---

[111] Except for my experience at age seventeen.

Appearances in writing

When I was little my grandmother would give me five dollars for every book that I read, but that still wasn't enough to make me do it more than a couple times. Things changed when I was thirteen, to the point that I'm surprised I don't wear quarter-inch-thick glasses now. Despite reading a ton, though, I have still only come across a few examples of this type of experience in writing. The English language does have a word for it also—*epiphany*—but that term has been misused enough that I won't use it.

No author that I have found has talked about the experience more than C.S. Lewis. The central theme of his autobiography, *Surprised by Joy*, is something he, fittingly, called "Joy." That experience, which he felt to be important enough to title the story of his whole life after, was this kind of event where we approach real knowledge and feeling. Lewis described the first time he had encountered that higher awareness, when he was just a child:

> As I stood beside a flowering currant bush on a summer day there suddenly arose in me without warning, and as if from a depth not of years but of centuries, the memory of that earlier morning at the Old House when my brother had brought his toy garden into the nursery. It is difficult to find words strong enough for the sensation which came over me...before I knew what I desired, the desire itself was gone, the whole glimpse withdrawn, the world turned commonplace again...it had taken only a moment of time; and in a certain sense everything else that had ever happened to me was insignificant in comparison.[112]

He also relates another experience that happened soon after, saying that it was, "the same surprise and the same sense of

---

[112] C.S. Lewis, *Surprised by Joy: The Shape of my Early Life* (San Diego: Harcourt Brace Jovanovich, Publishers, 1955), 16.

incalculable importance. It was something quite different from ordinary life and even from ordinary pleasure; something, as they would say, 'in another dimension.'"[113]

Other than Lewis, Plotinus (204-270 AD) has written more about this experience than anyone I've found, and his description is poignant:

> It has happened often. Roused into myself from my body — outside everything else and inside myself—my gaze has met a beauty wondrous and great. At such moments I have been certain that mine was the better part, mine the best of lives lived to the fullest, mine identity with the divine. Fixed there firmly, poised above everything in the intellectual that is less than the highest, utter actuality was mine. But then there has come the descent, down from the intellection to the discourse of reason. And it leaves me puzzled. Why this descent?[114]

"Why this descent?" I think we stay down in the dark with rare glimpses of proper human functioning and perception partly because we are dominated by our physical nature.[115] Or, even if our spiritual nature was to dominate instead, we would still be deeply broken and malfunctioning so that we would not see or feel right anyway. Plotinus answers his own question later also: "Why does a soul that has risen to the realm above not stay there? Because it has not yet entirely detached itself from things here below."[116] I suppose.

---

[113] Lewis, 17.

[114] Plotinus, *Enneads*, IV.8, 1.

[115] I should make it clear maybe at this point that I am not a mystic and I think that most of that kind of stuff has no foundation, does no good, and does not get anyone anywhere. What people need is to be forgiven for their sins, and meditating or studying isn't going to do that. But truth is truth and whatever this experience is, it is no illusion.

[116] Plotinus, *Enneads*, VI.9, 10.

Plato also addressed this form of knowledge and its fleeting nature. Plotinus was an Academic, meaning he held most of Plato's views, and he summarized Plato's views this way:

> Everywhere he holds the bodily in low esteem; he deplores the association of soul with body; he says that the soul is enchained and entombed by the body...What he calls 'the cave' seems to me, like the 'grotto' of Empedocles, to signify the realm of sense, because for the soul 'to break its chains and ascend' from its cave is, he says, to rise 'to the intelligible realm.' In *Phaedrus* 'the loss of its wings' is cause of the soul's descent; periodically recurring cycles bring the soul back down here after it has gone aloft. [117]

Back down to the cave. It's not a bad description.

The Republic is where Plato gives that famous passage about life in the cave,

> Behold! Human beings living in an underground den, which has a mouth open towards the light and reaching all along the den; here they have been from their childhood, and have their legs and necks chained so that they can not move, and can only see before them, being prevented by the chains from turning round their heads.[118]

He was not discussing exactly the same thing as I have been here, and I do not agree with a lot of his thought, but it is still very similar.

The trigger

So, we grope along in the dark usually, but what is it that triggers the intense flashes of life? From what I've read, there seems to be no telling what might suddenly cause the curtain inside us to

---

[117] Plotinus, *Enneads*, IV.8, 1.

[118] Plato, *The Republic*, book VII, page 1.

be lifted, or when it might happen. For Robert Leckie it was the threat of harm or death, at least on one occasion. Leckie was a Marine in World War 2 and in his book *Helmet for my Pillow* he described his first landing on an island (where he expected to be fighting and possibly dying):

> I no longer prayed. I was like an animal: ears straining for the sound of battle, body tensing for the leap over the side. The boat struck the shore, lurched, came to a halt. Instantly I was up and over. The blue sky seemed to swing in a giant arc. I had a glimpse of palm fronds swaying gently above, the most delicate and exquisite sight I have ever seen.[119]

Leckie's senses were heightened, adrenaline was flowing, and his heart was beating quickly. All those physical things played a part, but I think some other aspect of him came alive also that enabled him to appreciate life and to experience this: "*the most delicate and exquisite sight I have ever seen.*" ...Palm fronds.

Similarly, Michael Shaara described in the book *Killer Angels*: "dimly you could hear the music and the drums, and then you could hear the officers screaming, and yet even above your own fear came the sensation of unspeakable beauty."[120] He wasn't at Gettysburg, of course, but he had probably read firsthand accounts with similar descriptions, and had probably experienced such things enough times for himself in various life situations to paint an accurate image.

Dangerous and dramatic situations can cause a moment of real sight and feeling inside some people, but it was something else for Lewis.[121] He says that after the first time he experienced "Joy,"

---

[119] Robert Leckie, *Helmet for my Pillow* (New York: ibooks, 2001), 58.

[120] Shaara, Killer Angels, 341-42.

[121] Lewis fought in World War I, so if danger had affected him in this way, he would have had plenty of opportunity to experience it. He never mentions any such event in his autobiography, though, allowing a safe conclusion that danger was not an avenue for him.

during his boyhood—living in the cave without a single glance out of it—"This long winter broke up in a single moment," happening when he read a particular phrase of literature. As he describes,

> with that plunge back into my own past there arose at once, almost like heartbreak, the memory of Joy itself, the knowledge that I had once had what I had now lacked for years, that I was returning at last from exile and desert lands to my own country...I now stared round that dusty schoolroom like a man recovering from unconsciousness.[122]

Lewis's experience was almost always triggered by reading—by a particular literary genre even at that. He bought books of that type and says that the experience happened repeatedly through them.[123] He also mentioned that he met a schoolmate who said he got the same feeling from the same exact literature.[124]

Nature has never affected me powerfully, but it is another avenue that has caused some other people to come alive for a moment. It's not hard to imagine that looking into the wonder of the cosmos and at the largeness of the world could make something happen to some people on occasion. A friend of mine that I knew had not had the best time in his youth or in school, once told me that the first time he'd ever been west and seen the mountains from a distance, that he had cried. I could understand what he was talking about and why it might have done that to him. Life is bigger than the devilish little things that can dominate our world. At the same time that it is horrible, it is also magnificent; beyond the petty, the ugly, and the weak that characterizes so much of human interaction. The stars and the particles and the wild have no fear or guilt. They have never cringed, betrayed, or failed. And it's easy to accept the

---

[122] Lewis, 73.

[123] Lewis, 78.

[124] Lewis, 130.

possibility that if we truly saw and felt that something so massive exists and that it is absolutely impervious to the things that disturb and dominate us, that it could free us for an instant too.

I've personally tried to appreciate things like the picture taken by the Hubble telescope of thousands of little galaxies, and have done some gazing at stars and planets with an attempt to appreciate, but I've never been affected that much by any of it. Ansel Adams was, though. The veil was pulled back for an for him as he was hiking out west in the summer of 1923. He says,

> I was climbing the long ridge, west of Mount Clark. It was one of those mornings where the sunlight is burnished with a keen wind and long feathers of cloud move in a lofty sky. The silver light turned every blade of grass and every particle of sand into a luminous metallic splendor. There was nothing, however small, that did not clash in the bright wind; that did not send arrows of light through the glassy air. I was suddenly arrested in the long crunching path of the ridge by an exceedingly pointed awareness of the light. The moment I paused, the full impact of the mood was upon me. I saw more clearly than I have ever seen before or since the minute detail of the grasses, the small fotsam of the forest, the motion of the high clouds streaming above the peaks. I dreamed that for a moment time stood quietly, and the vision became but the shadow of an infinitely greater world. And I had within the grasp of consciousness a transcendental experience.[125]

The narrator of the show this was on commented aptly that Adams, "would spend the rest of his life trying to capture on film the quicksilver light he saw that morning, and the sense it conveyed of a deeper truth and meaning."

---

[125] Quoted from *Ansel Adams – A Documentary Film* (2002, PBS) by Ric Burns.

It's us

So, nature sweeps some people up occasionally, and danger affects others, but there is nothing so special about bullets and adrenaline or rocks and trees in themselves.

Nature, for example, is nice sometimes, but to the reasonable eye, the bare facts are that the hills are just rocks and dirt arranged completely randomly, and the surface of the earth really is crust and nothing more—arbitrary crumpled up cracks with a green organic layer on some of it like mold on a penny that could all be scraped off and smoothed out. Random crags—the mountains and the Grand Canyon and all the rest of it. Lewis had been brought into the intense feeling by the outdoors a time or two, but he also mentions that "even when real clouds or trees had been the material of the vision, they had been so only by reminding me of another world; and I did not like the return to ours."[126]

Likewise, I seem to be sensitive to departing the world for a moment during the day, but I don't consider there to be anything magical about sleeping during the day. Whatever it is that happens to trigger these experiences, the important thing is *us*. But there doesn't seem to be anything so magical about nature, as there's nothing magical about danger or daytime naps.

The important thing is what these externals do to the viewer. I had said earlier that without a feeling and conscious entity to observe its surroundings, nothing in existence would have any meaning. The haphazard rocks, holes, and vapors mean nothing on their own. But it might not be meaningless or coincidental that they can affect us, or that we can regard them as beautiful. So, some people are caught up by a phrase of Norse literature, some by sleeping at odd times, and there's no telling what might do this for others. It is not always the same for any one individual, and it also seems to vary between people. Neither nature, words on a page,

---

[126] Lewis, 181.

vibrations of air molecules called "music," or any other physical circumstance are what hold the real value. The feeling spirit is in us.

Rarity

It's clear in Lewis's narrative, though, that these flashes were also rare for him as they were for Plotinus. They are also rare for me and almost surely they are for everyone else in this world. Lewis said that after having the first several of them, for example, he entered a period still in his boyhood where "For many years Joy (as I have defined it) was not only absent but forgotten."[127] And he says that "Joy had vanished from my life: so completely that not even the memory or the desire of it remained." For many *years* Lewis had no experience or even memory of it.

I haven't had any such experience for maybe a decade. Actually, unless I've forgotten one—and they are not the kind of thing anyone would forget—the last instance was the one I described above, at age twenty…thirteen years ago.

They are rare, as precious things usually are, but it still seems that there must be something that would incline or disincline a person to be able to experience this taste of life. For instance, I don't think that anyone who is concerned only with impressing others, rather than with his own opinion of himself, or someone who has one face to show at one time and another for another time, will ever be in a position to really feel or appreciate anything. Thucydides said, "The key to happiness is freedom, and the key to freedom is a brave heart."—a brave heart, not a two-faced, chicken heart. It's certain that those who do not keep things straight inside themselves will have less capacity for life and experience, and will probably also have less chance of any glimpse outside the cave.

---

[127] Lewis, 34.

I also seem to have experienced these things more when I was young. What it takes to truly be alive is to be able to truly feel, but our capacity to feel is usually damaged by life and by our nature. We didn't even start out with full ability since we were born malfunctioning; but I do remember that as a child I could feel more, and at that time I knew and understood some things a lot better than I ever have since—as I mentioned chapters back. The young are still hopeful for what experience in life can be like, and for what the world might hold in store. And this pertains to this topic because, "Everything is possible for him who believes" (Mark 9:23). If an individual does not believe something is possible, it probably will not be possible for him. Young people might typically not have experienced enough pain and boredom yet to have all the hope squashed out of them for what could be, so they might believe that more could happen, allowing them to experience life more fully; for better or worse.

Could we live with this real sight?

These events are powerful and meaningful, but another question to ask is what their role could be in human life, when their frequency and duration is like shooting stars? Or, what could life be like if we could sustain the sight we gain in those moments? What if we could keep them? And, what if we could understand and see clearly, on a continual basis?

There are two considerations that answer those questions. The first one is that we don't seem to ever be able to stay in any experience for long; so our efforts probably aren't going to sustain the events. The second thing to consider is that we should be careful what we wish for, because if we were truly aware, and could truly see, feel, and understand our circumstances, and what happens in this existence, we would be crushed.

As just a lower caliber example describing that, I can say that I have heard people wishing for a more eternal perspective, and wondering how to get it. I could describe exactly how to do that, but not many people would like what they would see. If someone removes all his distractions for a week and goes without food for just a couple days, I guarantee that he will have a much clearer perspective on his own mortality, and of the real desperation and precariousness of the world. That is not a pleasant realization, and it can be overwhelming, but it's produced by just a couple simple efforts entirely within our own tiny powers. If the veil over reality was actually removed so that we could truly see for more than a moment, we would break down and come apart. We wouldn't be fit to work or converse with other people, or to operate at all in life.

I've encountered one passage describing this same conclusion, where Dallas Willard describes our lack of sight to be a defense mechanism,

> The mind preserves its own ability to stay on balance and carry on by denying, refusing to look at or be conscious of, things awful enough to paralyze us. The full horror of actual human behavior is like the face of the Medusa in Greek mythology. We sense that if we look squarely at it we will be turned to stone.[128]

I agree with this for the most part; although I don't think that we have any choice about our blindness, or that it's simply a defense mechanism.

Either way, even if we did have genuine sight, responding properly to it would be equally beyond any member of our frail species. Genuine realization happened to me that day when I was seventeen, for example, and even though I knew later on that same day that God had saved me and that I was safe, if the sight I'd been given hadn't also been removed, I would not have been able to go on living in any productive way. Our ignorance and the veil over our

---

[128] Dallas Willard, *The Spirit of the Disciplines* (San Francisco: HarperSanFrancisco, 1988), 224.

minds protects us. Only God can handle real understanding and only he can feel and see properly. Feeling as we aught to would destroy anyone else.

Conclusion

I described over several chapters that we do not understand, know, or appreciate. This is obvious enough that no rational person would deny it. We possess the factual knowledge, for example, that we're on a spinning sphere out in the universe, but we really do not grasp the fact. Or, we possess the factual knowledge that lots of kids don't have medical care or food, and that we're all going to die, but we don't appreciate those things or feel properly about any of them either.

I would like for my understanding and emotions to operate closer to correctly, but I don't have any unreal expectations of ever being the way a correctly functioning creature should be — sometimes described as "perfect." We are all very broken, and that is just the way it is. In addition, I would not say that more of those flights into the higher experience would really help in daily life.

What those events do provide, though, is some insight into what real knowledge, understanding, and meaning are. They are also strong evidence that those things are not achieved solely through our ability to reason. Knowledge is more than possession of facts. There is a big part of it that is feeling and spirit.

Conclusion on Knowing, Understanding, and Feeling

In the area of knowledge, I think I could say fairly of myself, and not even as a joke, that I am a man of science. I dislike superstition and could give plenty of examples of superstition in action that raise the hair on my neck and make my lip curl up a little. But I am still convinced that the most important things in life extend to places much higher than logic will ever be able to reach, and that there is often no explanation for them.

A lot of people would propose that all of those mysterious things are as mundane and corporeal as everything else, though; especially that the flights to an awareness and feeling beyond the natural are simply physical, chemical conditions of the brain. But when a person actually experiences one of those events, he knows better than that, and he has no doubts.

Our deepest knowledge

Based on all of my experience, doubts can and will come, but not during those moments. Usually everything is uncertain in life, but at those times when the veil is lifted back, there *is* complete certainty and the individual knows about whatever he sees a lot better than any scientist or experiment or tool of logic ever could. At those times he is looking *down* at that lower plane where reason operates as our primary, and often our only guide, and where we live every day. There is no comparison between the power of the two.

Through five chapters I described our dark condition here, and our incurable and ubiquitous uncertainty. But our uniquely human way of knowing is real and it is superior to reason, as Plotinus agreed:

> the act and faculty of vision is not reason but something greater than, prior and superior to, reason....Therefore it is so very difficult to describe this vision, for how can we represent as different from us what seemed, while we were contemplating it, not other than ourselves but perfect at-oneness with us?[129]

The vision he is describing here is not physical vision, but is vision by something else. It seems clear that Plato, Plotinus, and all those of their school of thought were led to at least a substantial part of their philosophy and religion by personal experiences where they were moved. When it happens there's a knowledge more powerful than reason can provide, and this is why Plotinus described it as, "greater than, prior and superior to."

Others have also said that our ability to know through this un-named avenue is higher than knowledge through logic. Will Durant describes Kant, for example, as a man "who was groping his way out of the darkness of atheism, and who boldly affirmed the priority of feeling over theoretical reason."[130] This is very surprising, considering that Kant was the supremely rational man. Some of the people who knew him said that Kant had a "cold or even frozen heart," he wrote works with titles like this one: "On the Power of the Mind to Master the Feeling of Illness by Force of Resolution," his schedule was so rigorous that it was said that women around the town he lived in could set their clocks by his daily walk, and reason

---

[129] Plotinus, *Enneads*, VI.9, 10.

[130] Durant, *Story of Philosophy*, 261.

was the chief virtue and guiding light in most of his writing. Nevertheless, Kant seemed to have recognized a valid ability within us to discern truth by some means other than logic.

Hume also agrees that feeling is a valid guide, even if he does not see it as superior to reason. One expert describes that Hume "advanced beyond scepticism in the name of feeling and the view that feeling not reason (reason being but a variant of feeling) is what *truly* discloses to us the real."[131] The romantics such as Jacques Rousseau also believed in the superiority of feeling over intellect, of course, and the philosopher G.E. Moore (1873-1958) said that one can know things without proof, otherwise it would be impossible to know anything, since each proof always depends on something that is *known* already or taken for granted.[132]

I believe that the human, feeling, insights are the most powerful form of knowledge that we are capable of. Part of the evidence for this is that they include more than just certainty, such as we have in knowing that the Pythagorean Theorem is true, but they also include *understanding* and a grasp of meaning, which makes them greater than plain certainty or knowledge. I'm also confident in every one of these glimpses of reality that I have had, and I would trust that most of them that other people describe are real as well.

Powerful, but not a cure

Aside from divine revelation, these events are the most powerful knowledge our species can have. But they are not a cure for our condition here. Our chronic uncertainty and blindness remain, the glimpses are always brief, and no one could come up with a set of doctrines from them. Excluding what I saw when I was seventeen, all that I could specifically derive from my experiences

---

[131] Milbank, *Hume Versus Kant*, 279.

[132] Charles Landesman, *An Introduction to Epistemology* (Cambridge: Blackwell, 1997), 68.

would be, maybe, that the world is insane, that we are spiritual creatures, and that reason doesn't give us an idea of the largest things that exist. Those are truths worth realizing, but they're not enough to guide anyone through life. A worldview made from just those ideas would still need a lot of work, since the most important questions would still be left unanswered. Aside from that one day for me at age seventeen—which was an entirely different type of experience from what I've been addressing here—all of these events are glimpses into what true understanding and feeling really are, but they are not teachers or books on truth. They also can't be repeated by us at will, and they are subject to doubt later, whereas logic can be repeated at any time, or written revelation could be read at any time. Because of these factors, these experiences are not a cure for our problem of uncertainty.

Our last avenue to truth

We all suffer because of our uncertainty, whether we usually recognize it or not. But I can still mention one last avenue to knowledge that I think is the most important one, and that every human being has access to. It is *conviction*; or simply knowing without being able to explain how or why.

This ability doesn't require a flight above regular awareness to operate, and everyone has it. I think that anyone who has been alive for a little while would also probably be able to think of examples of this kind of knowledge or intuition from his or her own life where he knew, but could not say *how*. I have experienced it most clearly in relation to the New Testament, where I simply know that it is true. And I consider that sense of truth to be a more certain form of knowledge than logic alone could produce about any religious issue. Compared to those flashes of awareness when my head got above the clouds for a moment, or compared to the conviction of truth that I have felt about particular things, everything else that I've ever thought or heard has been like bits of data stored on a lifeless computer—uncertain and meaningless.

We remain mostly in the dark with only a couple matchsticks of light, but in the future things will not be the way they are now, one way or another. If there is no God and the clock keeps turning like it has, the sun will expand and bake the earth to ashes, and it will all be gone. ...That would settle things. No more uncertainty then. But if there is a God, and the Bible is true, it stands to reason that after we leave these bodies God will restore proper functioning to those people who have decided they want to know him, so that their whole life will be like those brief moments of real life that we experience here. Then we will know and see. The uncertainty will finally be gone.

Now we see but a poor reflection as in a mirror; then we shall see face to face. Now I know in part; then I shall know fully, even as I am fully known (1 Cor. 13:12).

Happiness, the Elusive

The issue of belief and certainty has been covered. For a few chapters now I'll describe the other topic that interests me most, and then be finished.

The foremost goal of every human being is to feel good. Usually that quest is phrased as the desire for happiness rather than feeling, but the meaning is the same, since happiness is composed of feelings. I already described the importance of feeling to life—that without it there would be no meaning to anything, and really there would be no life, but just bodies moving around and electrons vibrating in brains. Without feeling also, the words *happiness, joy, peace,* or *fulfillment* wouldn't even have definitions, and anything else that we might seek would become useless as well.

It makes sense, then, that our highest goal is a set of feelings, and it's generally agreed on today, as it has been throughout history, that this is our final objective in almost everything we do. Nicholas Smith, for example, summarized that, "Most of the ancient Greek philosophers up through and including Aristotle conceived of the aim or goal of human life, or the highest human good, as *eudaimonia*—typically translated as 'happiness,' but which some have also translated as 'human flourishing.'"[133] A lot of the things that we pursue might appear to have other objectives as their end, but, in

---

[133] Smith, *Ancient*, 49.

reality, those other things aren't sought for their own sake, but only for the sake of the happiness that we think they'll provide.[134]

As a couple examples of this, I could point out that we don't want to make a decent amount of money because we like the green and white paper, and we don't want to live somewhere nice because we like clean paint, grass, and nice tiles for their own sake. We want those things because of the *happiness* or the good feelings we hope they will give us, either directly or indirectly. Badgers like living in holes and they would be unhappy in a penthouse. If the average human happened to like living in a dump instead of a nice place, then doing whatever we had to in order to secure a nice dump to live in (like the place I live in right now, for example) would become our surface goal, but the real objective would still be the same in either case—happiness. Those feelings are what we really desire in the end, and there's essentially nothing that we do where they are not the final objective. Pascal agreed with this also, describing our pursuit this way:

> All men seek happiness. There are no exceptions. However different the means they may employ, they all strive towards this goal. The reason why some go to war and some do not is the same desire in both, but interpreted in two different ways. They will never take the least step except to that end. This is the motive of every act of every man, including those who go and hang themselves.[135]

Even people who run out and risk being killed or wounded in a battle do it because they would rather risk that than to *feel* the

---

[134] Aristotle himself pointed out that an end that's pursued "for its own sake is more complete than that which is pursued for the sake of something else," and that "happiness is thought to be such an end most of all, for it is this that we choose always for its own sake" (*Nicomachean Ethics*, book 1, 5, 1097a, vs. 30).

[135] Pascal, X, 148. Pascal wrote more about happiness—and more usefully—than any other author I have seen, by far.

way they would forever afterward if they cowered. Or those that kill themselves would rather feel nothing, or face whatever is beyond, than to continue feeling the pain that they do now, or that they anticipate for the future in life. And those that sacrifice for another person do so for the sake of feelings, because they would rather bear pain or consequences themselves, than to bear the feeling they would have from knowing what the other was facing or had suffered if they hadn't helped.

So these feelings are our objective, and this goal is simple, but none of us is unfamiliar with the difficulty of being able to actually reach it. We pursue happiness our entire lives in one form or another, but it is fast, elusive, and slippery. What exactly is it that keeps us from ever grasping it? Approaching that question in a rigorous way won't lead to a new formula that scientists could draw up for us and then build into some machine or drug to solve our quest, but I have found that recognizing our condition can still bring a measure of peace, so I'll describe the layout of the obstacle course that no one ever seems to be able to get through.

Obstacles to happiness

Obviously, sickness and injury are two things that keep a lot of people from happiness or contentment. Those who are sick or have some other physical problem will have quite a bit of trouble feeling alright in this world, no matter how good their attitude is. And if they could be offered a deal so that they could live forever in the conditions they live in now, not many of them would take it. I don't think many people at all would take that deal if they understood what it would mean, no matter how good things are for them in this world relative to others.

A second obstacle to happiness is that, sick or not, knowing that we're going to get old and rickety, hunched over, and not able to do anything, then to die, puts a damper on the party at all times, usually even for those who are confident of a reception in heaven. We cannot completely forget about the dire straights of one kind or another that we're approaching, even during a picnic in the sun. The specter of the end that will strike us is always there in our subconscious.

A third thing that keeps us from happiness is our uncertainty, and I described what we suffer because of it in earlier chapters. If everything else in the world was good, the fact that we don't know what this world is about might actually not bother us that much and might not be such a cause of distress and turmoil. However, given the pain that does exist in the world, it is crucial to us to possess some degree of certainty, and this is obvious any time people suffer. In pain or difficulty people who didn't seem to care about truth before start grasping desperately, trying to figure things out and trying to find answers. Our condition and the nature of this world, though, prevent us from consistent, real certainty, and, thus, from happiness also.

Having to work all the time doesn't help us along in our quest for happiness either. Work and the requirements of getting by are probably the most widespread and constant of all external obstacles to being happy in this world. Amazingly, though, this problem would actually have to be explained to some people who are from a more fortunate background. Because of that, I'll diverge for a minute to describe this obstacle a little bit.

The work obstacle

I didn't fully realize until I got to be about thirty that I was born to some privilege. My parents shared one beat up old junker car until I was about twelve, and we turned the heat off at night in the winter to save money, etc. But I never had to worry about being cared for, never went without anything, and I was in school until age twenty-five—far removed from the real nature of the fight against starvation that most humans have to face year after year like a deer in winter. I think about things too much for my own good, and I have a pretty good idea of a lot of situations that I've never personally experienced, but it's still hard for people who've been fortunate to comprehend what life is like for those who have to toil, and it took me a while to be able to actually see it. Darwin described this ignorance, saying that "it is difficult to believe in the dreadful but quiet war of organic beings, going on in the peaceful woods, & smiling fields."[136] If you look at the field without considering what's really going on in it, it looks nice, and with a moderate amount of money or a diverting enough job, the world might look fairly nice too. In good conditions the brutal bottom line of our species' existence here is masked, and those who are dealt a more fortunate hand in life will probably never comprehend that there is a "dreadful but quiet war" going on in the cities and road crews and low-wage jobs; lifelong, every single week, until our bodies die. A lot of fortunate people are oblivious to that fact.

This is evident in some of the messages heard from our culture that are in movies, books, schools, stickers, posters, and other places. Most of the messages are true, but they are grossly incomplete, and the part that's left out indicates the prosperity of the culture that came up with them. "Happiness doesn't lie in possessions," for example, is a true saying that we like a lot. But that thought leaves out a huge piece of the real truth because it's a pretty safe bet that *un*happiness *does* lie in poverty. Our cultural wisdom also teaches that "happiness isn't found in career climbing" which is also true. But the part left out there is that *un*happiness *would* be found stamping one fold into a metal casing on an assembly line 40 hours a week as a career. Or, if there was no unhappiness yet with that job, we could make it digging ditches for seventy hours a week,

---

[136] From Darwin's journal, 1839.

and, then, a better job and more money *would* mean something closer to happiness.

Jack London took a good look at the full truth and at what work does to us when he dressed as a pauper and lived in the slums of London for two months. He described what he saw in *The People of the Abyss*, and what's written in that book is bad to the point that it's hard to believe. I can remember lying down to sleep the night I finished it, thinking about what I'd read, and about this world in general, and then simply crying. I've cried, I think, four times in my life as an adult, and that was one of them, and it seemed very strange, but also appropriate. The coldness and brutality of our world isn't lost on me, and weeping is pretty much the only thing to do when it comes down to it. There is no answer for this place except for God to put it to an end.

One of London's comments that might make a good summarizing statement of his observations was this: "with life so precarious, and opportunity for the happiness of life so remote, it is inevitable that life shall be cheap and suicide common....Poverty, misery, and fear of the workhouse, are the principle causes of suicide among the working classes."[137] A life of toiling for survival *crushed* people, and a lot of them took the only exit available from it. And only the most ignorant of us would say that they were unethical or irrational for it. What the world was like for them, and what it guaranteed to continue being like for them through the remainder of their days, made it the most logical option.

East London during Jack London's time was a particularly bad situation, but that situation existed in this very same world that we live in now, and there are plenty of similar conditions around the world today, as there always have been. Immigrants that make it up here from South America, for example, leave their homes, wives and children, risk their lives, and hide in trucks for days at a time with no

---

[137] Jack London, *The People of the Abyss* (London: Pluto Press, 2001), 142.

food because of *work*. Toiling sixty hours a week in their home countries, just to be able to survive, makes for a miserable life that they will do whatever they possibly can to escape from.

The pain of work is also not exclusive to those in the worst situations, though. It's at least a hindrance to happiness for almost all of us, for almost all of our lives. For myself, I know that when I got the flu after a few years on the job with no letup, I was genuinely glad because it meant a break, finally. Maybe not many people would welcome physical ailments for that reason, but there are still not many people that don't at least look forward to retirement, or wish the weekend would last indefinitely. Even if work is not a burden heavy enough to completely squelch the hope of a happy life out of us—as it has been for most people for most of history—it is at least a hindrance to us experiencing our goal of happiness in life.

So there's the obstacle of work. It's the most common external problem for our happiness, but it's still only one of many.

The final obstacle

Outside circumstances are the reason for a lot of our discontent and unhappiness—the ones described above and countless others, like, for example, having disproportionately large and clumsy feet like my friend Becky. But even if we could fix all outside circumstances—solve all medical problems, bring peace to earth, prove that there is a God who cares about us, cure physical aging and death, and not even have to work for food, but live in some Star Trek utopia; *even then, we still would not be happy.* Life would be much better, but we would not be happy then either because external circumstances do not account for all of our pains in this life. The problems are outside of us, and they are also *inside* of us, and this is why we are still discontent even when all of our outside circumstances are great.

Even if we could fix the war-torn, disease ravaged, impoverished places in the world, for example, we would then just be welcoming those nations to what *we* have—quiet desperation, anxiety, despondency. The rich aren't content either. Even those with good health, good looks, emotional stability, good company, wealth, and any other good things that could be imagined, aren't fulfilled either, because the problem is internal as well. "All men complain: princes, subjects, nobles, commoners, old, young, strong, weak, learned, ignorant, healthy, sick, in every country at every time, of all ages, and all conditions."[138]

Even when I was a child, and life was just a big playground, not everything was well internally, although I was very healthy in body and mind. I had never done anything to trouble my conscience, I had good parents, a big wheel bike, and everything else I could have wanted. I could describe conditions to have been just about perfect. But I still remember getting bored and not being able to be happy without something to do, and I can remember wanting to go to California because I thought that somehow life was different and better there. A lot of the world still has a similar dream about America.[139] Also, several times in childhood, a deep loneliness and feeling that something was very wrong came over me. I was happy relative to the rest of the world's condition, but there are problems built into the human being, and they will make themselves known in the way we feel. All is not well, even in a good childhood, and our problems only seem to grow and get stronger along with our bodies.

It's obvious in that example and plenty of others that even those people for whom everything is perfect do not have fulfillment. The best of the best aren't happy either. Those who would be at the

---

[138] Pascal, X, 148.

[139] "Life is not always good here, and we have problems, but in *America* life is great...if I can only get to America." *There*, in *that* place, things are good. I've heard immigrants to this country say that they had that very idea, and that they were disillusioned when they arrived here.

head of the class as far as fortune and blessings are also hoping to just get through this thing. The kids who did their homework in high school, never veered off what society says is the good path, then went to college and did all they were supposed to do there, and are working their good job, married to a good wife, and who sent their kids off to good colleges...they aren't happy either. They come home from work and watch TV to distract themselves from how they feel, and they find something to fill every hour of every weekend so they don't have to face their internal condition, and eternity, just like everyone else. Life will often be more enjoyable for the fortunate than for people who have to work, or certainly than for those who are sick, but other problems can come to life in place of the more common external ones, and grab those who are very fortunate. Fear of loss, domination by possessions, or greed might be a few of them.

This verse was not badly said:

> I have seen another evil under the sun, and it weighs heavily on mankind: God gives some people wealth, possessions and honor, so that they lack nothing their hearts desire, but God does not grant them the ability to enjoy them
> (Eccl. 6:1-2).

Let's try to overcome ourselves then

So, given all of this, we arrive at the great lesson that happiness doesn't lie in health, money, or other physical things. And, in fact, that idea is actually a popular mantra in society. Our culture often recognizes that good external conditions don't automatically produce happiness, and we're intrigued by stories of individuals who had all of the best things at one time but then left it all in order to live in a cave or wander the earth or something like that. We admire something about those types of people, and something about their actions stirs a desire in us. Individuals like that have realized that external conditions are not the last obstacle to fulfillment—again, as many of us have—but *they* have taken extreme actions to find happiness.

The attempt is admirable. But something that I have figured out, and can promise, is that those who leave their riches for the cave or the desert are going to find out that they still aren't happy, and that they will never fully overcome the remaining obstacle to happiness—their own nature. Those who realize that fortune and the admiration of millions, breaking world records and climbing ladders does not bring lasting happiness, and who give up the pursuit of all those things in order to focus on the internal, will find out that it's not so much fun to be left with themselves all the time either. Anyone who doubts that should try spending three days with no distractions, doing nothing, and see how they're feeling by the end. Monasteries, in fact, seem to me to be about the most miserable places in the world. Force yourself day after day to look at nothing but your own condition and, inevitably, at your separation from God, trying desperately to fix it…no thank you very much. I've tried that basic scenario before for years, determined to overcome, and it did the opposite of helping.

The way we respond to silence makes the problems that are inside us very obvious. "If man were happy, the less he were diverted the happier he would be, like the saints and God," Pascal said.[140] But we *aren't* happy, and if we have too much time with ourselves, we become even less so. We have to have something to do to distract us from our condition and from how we feel inside. Pascal continued:

> A man wealthy enough for life's needs would never leave home to go to sea or besiege some fortress if he knew how to stay at home and enjoy it. Men would never spend so much on a commission in the army if they could bear living in

---

[140] Pascal, VIII, 132.

town all their lives, and they only seek after the company and diversion of gambling because they do not enjoy staying at home....The only good thing for men therefore is to be diverted from thinking of what they are, either by some occupation which takes their mind off it, or by some novel and agreeable passion which keeps them busy, like gambling, hunting, some absorbing show, in short by what is called diversion. That is why gaming and feminine society, war and high office are so popular.[141]

We definitely don't want too much time with ourselves. Happiness doesn't lie there either, and there are some specific reasons for that. It's more difficult to identify the problems inside ourselves, whereas the external problems are obvious. But at least a couple of the internal ones are clear.

Our moral failure is one. I found out when I was young that even if we see clearly what we should be like, and then make our uttermost best effort to be that person, and live that way, we will still be resounding failures. We are hateful or we are cowardly or we are selfish. And we're probably all of those things in our own unique mixture of failure, every day.

And the reason that this matters for our happiness is that we have a conscience that can't be completely killed or drowned by any means, and it will make its existence known to us in how we feel. If someone acts badly he will also feel badly, at least to some extent. So it would be impossible to be happy without being morally straight. Aristotle said that, "happiness is not found in such pastimes [bodily pleasures] but in activities according to virtue."[142] Happiness is found according to our virtue. If somebody's behavior isn't up to par, there is no way he could be free, and there is no way that he

---

[141] Pascal, VIII, 136.

[142] Aristotle, *Nicomachean Ethics*, book X, 1177a, vs 10.

would not feel accordingly. We wonder how some people can live with themselves, and I think that, in truth, it is not easy for them. But the shortcomings in our moral behavior is in us all.

Another obstacles inside ourselves is our unique human flaws, which we are all guaranteed to have gotten a share of. Some people think badly of themselves. Some have bad anxiety. Some attach their personal value to how much other people like them. Some people are afraid of the future and the present. It's always something.

At this point, then, there are a couple conclusions, and a slight problem might seem to be taking shape: If we seek the feelings we want in the adulation of others, the bright-eyed girlfriend, the nice house on a hill, accomplishments, and a supercharged Corvette, we find that it's not there. *However*, if we conclude that we have to seek this happiness internally, we will find that it's not such a nice place inside ourselves either! No matter how circumstances are, and regardless of whether we turn inward or outward to fix what keeps us from happiness, we seem to remain discontent. And this helplessness is what causes us to always hope for the future.

Always the future

Very few people in this world, fortunate or unfortunate, would want for their current situation to last indefinitely, regardless of what that situation is. Everyone is looking forward to something in the future, because something in the present is painful or unpleasant, even if we can't quite put a name on what it is. Has that ever *not* been the case? For each living person there is also probably something that they're trying to overcome, and they are telling themselves that at this or that time, things will be better and that they will be able to rest. But that wish never comes true. It never turns out that way.

> All of our life passes this way: we seek rest by struggling against certain obstacles, and once they are overcome, rest proves intolerable because of the boredom it produces. We must get away from it and crave excitement. We think either of present or of threatened miseries, and even if we felt quite safe on every side, boredom on its own account would not fail to emerge from the depths of our hearts where it is naturally rooted, and poison our whole mind.[143]

Pascal was right in this, and Aristotle said, similarly, that, "happiness is thought to depend on leisure; for we toil for the sake of leisurely activity, and we are at war for the sake of peaceful activity."[144] But it never works. We think we'll be happy once we overcome whatever, but then after our great victory, after our labors are completed, and we sit down to our new joy...a few days of rest and we can barely stand being with ourselves. So we continue to pin our hopes on the future; always the future.

Dostoevsky portrayed this delusion in one of his characters:

> He would take her and they would leave at once for the edge of the world...Then a completely new life would start for them! Of that new, "virtuous" life...he would dream and daydream constantly, obsessively....like so many others under such circumstances, he believed in the magic of a change of place—just to get away from this spot, to be surrounded by different people, to be in a different situation, where everything would be new and different![145]

---

[143] Pascal, VIII, 136.

[144] Aristotle, *Nicomachean Ethics*, book X, chapter 7, 1177b, vs. 5.

[145] Fyodor Dostoevsky, *The Brothers Karamazov* (New York: Bantam Classics, 2003), 489.

"Like so many others." "If only _____ and _____" or "if I can get here or there, at last I'll be happy."

No one should think that our interminable discontent is limited to any problem, type of problem, to any particular attempt, type of attempt, or to any culture or time period either. That would be another naïeveté—"if only I had lived in this time period, or if only I lived in this other place or culture, *then*..." There was never any golden age of mankind when people were happy. There have been times and places—and there still are today—when and where people have been less *un*happy, but the nature of this existence we live in, and of mankind, has always been the same. Thousands of years ago, for example, Lucretius said that each individual goes on

> not knowing what he wants for himself, and always seeking to change location, as if he could put down his burden. The man who is sick and tired of his home often leaves his mansion, and then suddenly returns, since he feels things are not at all better outdoors. Driving his imported ponies he races to his country villa at top speed, as if rushing to bring help to a house on fire. He immediately starts yawning when he touches the threshold of his villa, or goes off into a heavy sleep and just tries to forget, or dashing off again he seeks to return to the city. Thus each person flees himself, but he cannot, of course, escape the one he flees, but clings to him unwillingly and hates him because he is sick and does not understand the cause of his disease.[146]

That's how it is for us all. It's always the future; always the carrot on the stick. "If I can only ____, then I'll be happy." "If ____ works out, and ____ ____, *then* things will be good." *Then...then* I might be happy. Fill in the blanks however you want;

---

[146] Lucretius, *On the Nature of Things*, book 3, vs. 1060.

it's always something—some problem blocking us from reaching happiness at last. And what*ever* that thing is; once it's gained or overcome, it never does what we had hoped it would. The promised land that we expect to arrive at some day in the future always recedes into the distance out of reach.

People go through life wondering and theorizing that the problem and the reason they aren't happy is this and that. "It's the government. If only the government was fixed and ___ and ___, then..." Or, "It was my parents. If they hadn't ___ and ___, then..." Or it's society and everybody *else* around us. We also think that if we just do this or move there, or get this job, or become involved with this person, or a thousand other creative combinations...*then* we'll be happy. We always look to *the future* as the time things will finally be good; never the present, because in the present there is always some kind of problem.

We are a poor deluded world. Suffice it to say that we will never be completely happy until we can fix ourselves in addition to fixing everything outside ourselves. Anyone who wanted to do so could forsake any distraction or entertainment and get to work on it. But after quite a few years of things being pretty much the same for us all—regardless of what external situations have worked out well or badly for each of us—and after considering the condition of people throughout history, wisdom might begin to tell us that things will probably *always* be this way. We will *never* get to the happy land.

And "things" probably always being the same means *us* being the same. The internal conditions that each of us has to live with now—ourselves—are those that we will basically always have to live with. People can improve and consciences can be cleared and God can be approached more closely so that our souls become a better home to us. But the problems inherent to the species will never change, and we will share in them unless we can transform ourselves to into some creature that is not a human.

However, I do want to say that, despite the hopeless tone of these ideas, it *is* still comforting to realize that not being able to attain happiness, the holy grail of the human race, is not a particular failure on anyone's part, and it's not for lack of trying. No one is somehow missing out on what everyone else has. These conclusions might seem to be depressing and not useful for anything, but it is a relief to accept things for what they are and to be able to rest. I think it is wise to strive to be happy, but also to be realistic about our condition in this world.

End-all of Happiness

After resolving that happiness isn't found in anything on earth, or within ourselves, as described in the last chapter, Christians will always conclude that it's found only in God. If there is any hope for us to be happy, it is indeed there in our creator. That idea is the main thing to be addressed in this chapter. (I'll assume in this chapter that the Christian God exists.) And, whether you like it or dislike it, dedicate your life to it, or reject it, there is nobody that should not want to hear what the most revered or trusted sources say about happiness. The historical foundation of western culture, upbringing, family, and education is the Bible, and it's influence has been so ingrained into our ethical beliefs, laws, and culture, that we can't even consciously notice it; like we barely ever notice that our heart is beating or that we have been breathing every minute of our lives.

Humanity's ultimate goal in life is called by several of the most revered words we have: *happiness, joy, peace, or fulfillment*, and it's important to clear up something about the meaning of those words now, because there are some common misconceptions. Many people try to create a differentiation between happiness and the other words. They attempt to define happiness to be a feeling that's fleeting, and that comes and goes, whereas the more traditionally revered words like peace or joy are taken to indicate things that are permanent, and that are somehow higher than feelings—as if they're of some different and better type. Everyone that I've heard make that attempt at distinctions, though, gives one or two illustrations and then they stop, content that they've cordoned off *happiness* as a shallow goal from the other words that carry more virtuous connotations.

The first thing to mention is that *happiness, joy, peace,* and *fulfillment* are *all* feelings. None of them is some kind of golden ethereal object, too spiritual to be associated with such an earthly thing as a feeling. There are a couple of idea that lead to that conclusion without leaving much room for doubt. The first is to ask how anyone would know that they had peace, for example, if they couldn't feel it? Is a notarized document handed to them? "You are hereby verified as being in possession of peace." And what value would peace have if a person couldn't even know that he had it? None. I described in an earlier chapter that the only way we can know that we believe something is through a feeling associated with that belief. Likewise, the *only way* that we know that we have peace, joy, or fulfillment, is through feelings. Peace, joy, or fulfillment actually *are* feelings, just as happiness is. And, happiness is not the only one of those that's subject to change. Each one of them fluctuates in our experience throughout life.

Another important consideration to mention at the start is that, no matter how we might try to break these things up and label them, feelings within us still can't always be neatly distinguished or categorized as being one thing or another. The important consideration in the end, anyway, is the overall feeling of a human being. And *happiness* is the best word we have to describe that overall feeling inside someone that includes elements from peace, connection to God, conscience, internal and external circumstances, and anything else with any effect. That is how the word *happiness* has usually been used in the American and English culture, and that is how I'll use it. So now the definitions are done.

Biblical teaching

In general, the Bible doesn't say much explicitly about happiness. The word appears four times in the NASB translation (translation; i.e., Greek to English, done by a particular group of translators), and none of those four instances are in the New Testament. In the NIV translation the word appears six times—twice in the New Testament, both instances in Matthew. The word *fullness* appears only a few times in the Bible in the context of how an individual could normally experience life, as does *joy*. Those small numbers indicate the same thing that anyone would pick up from reading through the christian texts, which is that, for the most part, there are not individual instructions describing how a human being's emotional state should be, or how he or she should experience life. The message of happiness, joy, or fullness in life, does exist in the Bible, but it isn't specifically detailed in the Old or New Testament.

What can be taken most accurately about happiness from the Bible is more of a sense of things rather than a detailed doctrine. But if a particular statement on the topic could be used, I think the best would be Ephesians 3:17-21. Of all passages, it comes closest to describing how happiness and the benefits of knowing the creator in this world should be. As it says, "I pray that you, being rooted and established in love, may have power…to grasp how wide and long and high and deep is the love of Christ, and to know this love that surpasses knowledge—that you may be filled to the measure of all the fullness of God" (Ephesians 3:17-19). The impression that this verse, and the rest of the Bible, gives is that Christians should be fulfilled in life and that this is God's desire for all human beings. It's also apparent from that verse that fullness will depend largely on us somehow grasping and experiencing God's love. But it also seems, from the fact that this passage is a prayer, that people could miss the fullness described. If something was definitely going to either happen or fail to happen, there would be no need to pray for it. The possibility that someone might fail to experience being "filled to the measure of all the fullness of God" (which we can see from experience to be the norm) is why Paul felt the need to pray that it would happen.

So, the biblical texts indicate that fullness of life or happiness are possible for anyone who believes in Jesus Christ. However, difficulty is also promised, with the associated pains. Those difficulties shouldn't remove the feelings of peace and joy that can be had, but they can overwhelm them. Being beaten and thrown in prison and reviled by everyone, for example, might tip the scales to make someone not be doing too well at all, either physically or mentally. Or, more realistically for us, being sick, having to work a miserable job, being naturally pessimistic, or being alone, despite otherwise good circumstances, might tip the scales to make us not be feeling so good either.

And I think it's important to realize that difficulties like these might tip the scales that way, *period*, despite the best attitudes, actions, or intentions of any of us. Even with the peace that transcends understanding and the "rich provision of everything for our enjoyment" on one side of the balance, the other side might have some pretty heavy issues on it too, and we may just not be doing so well. And if that's the case, it doesn't indicate some kind of personal failure. People should be realistic about these things.

The Christian answer: Happiness in God alone

The Bible has limited teaching on happiness in life, and its message on that topic is mostly implied rather than explicit. But the Christian culture does have an explicit teaching on happiness. I have assumed in this chapter that Jesus Christ is God. And, if this proposition is true, those people that act on that proposition, of all human beings, should have the best answers to our quest for happiness. They're the group who would know, if anyone does.

Christians will always conclude that fulfillment or happiness is only found in God. That is the most common Christian answer to the gigantic question of our species, and it is the answer that I have personally believed and depended on for a long time. Anyone who *would* believe that a deity created us for himself, would have to conclude the same thing. However, after a lot of thought and experience, I've learned that this answer has to be adjusted and qualified.

Of course it's true that our best and only hope of fulfillment and of feeling alright, at long last, is in God, but, unfortunately, we aren't happy or at peace with much consistency there either. Not in this world. This disappointment is not because of some shortcoming of God's, but it is reality, and it's an idea that isn't described much...actually it's another thing that I have never heard so much as a whisper of from anyone in my life, or seen one time in writing. I would say that it is a pretty important thing to realize, though, and the obscurity, or total absence of any discussion of it is why I feel it's important to describe here.[147]

If the accounts of Christ are true, then mankind was made to know the creator, and God has made that possible. For that reason, those that should have the most complete life are those that have taken advantage of a relationship with God. Those individuals should also be able to sit fourteen hours a day for years in a row without the need for distraction—as long as physical needs are met—enjoying their connection to God, who is the end-all of our

---

[147] I can imagine the surprise that would accompany a lot of statements that I make in this chapter and elsewhere. But until someone can show me that an inability to be at peace or to be feeling good in silence for a few days, or even for a few hours, doesn't indicate a major problem, and doesn't demonstrate that there is not great peace with God here in our experience, I'll stick to what I've said. Or if the person who thinks that God provides fulfillment completely and fully can go and spend just a few days in happy, and complete, isolation and solitude, and then report back that it was a real blast, I'll revisit my conclusions. It is definitely because of our failures that the individual who would try this wouldn't be able to do it happily, but is there anyone who doesn't fail in that exact way?

happiness. After all, he made human access to himself possible at the greatest possible cost, so it should be taken advantage of with the greatest enthusiasm and frequency. But there is a way that things *should* be, and then there is the way that they *are*, and those two are light-years away from each other.

I have known a lot of Christians over the last seventeen years and none of them could rest in silence for hours just being happy. Even the best person, who does everything he should and everything that anyone could, cannot sit "in his own room" as Pascal said, basking in the fulfillment he should have in God. *Un*-strangely enough, any other homo sapien, regardless of beliefs or background, will be about the same. About an hour of quiet thought might be alright, but any more than that and the creature starts to get restless. Essentially no one can be happy in God and nothing else all the time without going nuts within a short while, being bored to death, or becoming otherwise distraught. A biographer described that Martin Luther, for example, would sometimes pray for three days on end until he learned better. After one of those times, "For five days he could get no sleep, and lay on his bed as one dead, until the doctor gave him a sedative" and "during convalescence the prayer book revolted him."[148] But that should have been a really great time for him, right? Not so much. And, after a while, Luther learned better and gave up. Good thing he did.

There are a few exceptions to this rule—like I said, I hardly left my room for two months after first believing, and it was the best time of my life—but they are extremely rare. I certainly couldn't spend long stretches of isolated time now without being miserable.

---

[148] Roland Bainton, *Here I Stand: a Life of Martin Luther* (New York: Meridian, 1995), 152.

Why isn't God all we need?

To lay out the situation again: every man, woman, and child, wants to be happy in life, and each one seeks that end. But we do not find it. There are obstacles outside of ourselves that we can rarely overcome, and there are obstacles inside us that we can *never* overcome. The best answer and solution to this overarching desire of our existence is that God is the only thing that can make us happy—through a close connection to him. So, let every creature rejoice once more. But, to repeat also, I know from all of the personal accounts I've read, from all the people I've known, and from my personal experience, that the rule is that we do not find complete happiness in God either. So our final hope fails. *Why?*

It would be nice to have an answer to that question and to know what the problem is, since fixing stuff always begins with a diagnosis of what's wrong. I can say, in answer to that, that a lot the reason we rarely find happiness, even in God, is that he is distant from us. And there is a particular reason for that, in turn.

All of us will change and be diminished by circumstances we're around. We'll be influenced by our surroundings and become different people to some degree. Even if we know that something that has come into our presence is wrong, we will still start adjusting to make peace with it, because we aren't strong enough to deal with it, or because we're too scared, or because we can't recognize it, or because of some other failure. God isn't like that.

If the God of the Bible exists, he is impermeable, he is not influenced or intimidated, and if he is put in the presence of evil, it just isn't going to work. He doesn't get scared, he doesn't wonder if he might be off base, and he will not start to adjust himself to accommodate things the way that we do. Instead, he may very well just start destroying. Some of the strongest people in life, like kings, are described to be like forces of nature, and you better be careful around them. God is much more than a person. Certain chemicals react to each other in a particular way, and that's just what they do. Acetylene and oxygen will not be talked out of producing a flame. Pure things are pure, and their reactions are what they are.

If God does not react well to foul things, then it only stands to reason that the more hypocritical or hateful *we* are, or the further that we get into any other kind of dirt, the less that our final source of happiness would be able to let us be close to him. In *Exodus* he told Israel to go up to the land, but he said, "I will not go with you, because you are a stiff-necked people and I might destroy you on the way" (Exodus 33:3). And, "the LORD had said to Moses, 'Tell the Israelites, "You are a stiff-necked people. If I were to go with you even for a moment, I might destroy you"'" (Exodus 33:5).

It's very likely that we remain at a distance from God, and that he keeps himself at a distance from us, for a particular reason: *our survival*. Thus, our only possible source of real happiness is unreachable. In a way, this doesn't make sense, since, according to the Bible, those who believe are cleansed and covered by Christ's actions so that God regards them as clean. And, for example, it says that as a result of God making access to himself possible, Christians should, "draw near to God with a sincere heart in full assurance of faith, having our hearts sprinkled to cleanse us from a guilty conscience" (Hebrews 10:22). In Christianity, though, there is always "the already, but not yet."[149]

The strangeness of this situation is also apparent in particular passages. For example, Moses was not perfect either, yet it says that he talked with God face to face, whereas God declared that the other people had better not even set foot on the mountain, or they would die (Exodus 33:11, 19:13). God would speak with Moses face to face, but, basically, for everybody else, there would be a distance in their connection to God (Numbers 12:5-8). And it is honestly a pretty huge distance.

---

[149] The Bible recognizes this as well. For example, I Cor 13:12, 2 Cor 5:6-8.

So, somehow, God sees those who've received him as clean, and they can be close to him, but the more evil they have in them, the farther he has to be from them, since he just cannot be around it. "Who may ascend the mountain of the LORD?" it asks. "Who may stand in his holy place? The one who has clean hands and a pure heart" (Psalm 24:3-4). The one who has clean hands and a pure heart is the one that can be close to God, but none of us really achieves that in this world, so we will always be somewhat removed from him in this life, and, therefore, somewhat removed from happiness.

Because of this factor, the modified answer and conclusion on how we should reach for happiness is basically that we should try to be good. And there is some wisdom to this. Nobody is going to find much fulfillment and joy in their maker if they do as they please and make no effort; I believe that's one thing that is guaranteed. But I have also learned better by this time than to just take that philosophy and run with it, or to give it as a final line of advice.

The confounding thing is that, quite often, even if we almost bust a vein trying to do as we should and to be close to God, he may still be very distant in our experience so that we are unable to find much, if any, happiness there at all. We may find ourselves in this state, despite doing our very best. And we cannot "just" do any one thing or another, or "just" realize one thing or another that's going to fix it. A lot of people will make those claims of how easy it's supposed to be, but, in addition to the fact that they themselves probably have none of the goods that they're hawking, if it was a matter of "just" doing something or realizing something, everyone would do it and everyone would be happy in life.

If this frustrated effort towards happiness is true of someone who believes in Jesus Christ, and even they don't seem to be able to find a complete salve for their hurts or fulfillment to their yearnings in God, it might begin to look like something is seriously wrong. But that should not come as too much of a surprise, because something *is* seriously wrong. Lots of things are. I've described a lot of them at length in this book.

More problems

I mentioned our uncleanness as one problem, for example, but lists of moral offenses are not the whole reason that we are distant from our creator, or why trying to connect to him very often doesn't make us feel one little bit better. Another specific hindrance to our happiness is faith, or lack of it. It's unlikely that anyone could connect to our creator if they doubted the whole time that he even exists. And another hindrance could be (and very likely is) that an individual wasn't close to his own father and that he projects problems from there onto God. I was surprised to find myself doing that many years ago. A fourth reason for our distance from him is that we have an animal nature, as well as a spiritual one, that wants sex, food, video games, smokes, alcohol, entertainment, and other things for the eyes, ears, and sense of touch that are not found by us now in the one who's invisible. Those desires don't just die at any time in life, regardless of what happens to us or what we do, and they *will* distract us. We've probably all experienced how sexual attraction can subdue all other elements of our nature, or how an urge in our youth to go out on Friday night wouldn't allow anything else to carry any weight inside us. Battling with and suffering from ourselves in this way will never stop.

What should we do then to be happy, other than trying to be good? The central answer of Christians is still that "God is all you need," and I'll back up now and take another approach to examine the validity of that. The question begs to be asked right away: "God is 'all we need' for what exactly?" He is all we need in order not to be so depressed that we get to be suicidal? It's true that he is the first and biggest part of what we need to be fulfilled, but he is not *all* we need to be feeling and doing alright in life, unless extremely rare miraculous action by God is involved. I would give up anything that I have, including my health or my life, rather than lose Jesus Christ, but it has not proven to be true that he is all that I or any other member of the species needs to be close to happy in this world. Take away enough other stuff, and he's not all we need for that.

As would make sense, our creator does fulfill more than anything else, but usually not completely. Experience certainly supports this, and the Bible does as well. No matter how *Genesis* is interpreted, it makes that fact clear. That book implies that the first human being knew God and that he functioned perfectly as he was designed to.[150] He wasn't all messed up like all of us are, and the internal obstacles I've described to be in us weren't present in him. But God still said it wasn't good for him to be alone down on the earth. And there it is. Something was wrong and something was missing, even when an unspoiled connection to the maker existed. I don't see how that could not mean that God made man deliberately so that his relationship with him did not fulfill completely. If God had designed us to need him alone, the text would say that man was on his own, it was good, and that was that. So this is one support— God did not design us so that he is the only thing we need in this world to be happy.

More support comes from the example of a human being in prison. If the best and most godly person is put in a prison cell with bed, food, heat, and air, but he isn't happy or at peace with just those

---

[150] I'm not going to discuss the issue of evolution in any detail, but I will make just a couple comments. Based only on empirical evidence, including the fossil record, I believe it is very unlikely that we evolved out of bacteria in the ocean. Some people believe otherwise. But one thing is certain: nobody should be so ignorant as to think that a large degree of faith is not required on either side of the issue. Anyone who cares anything about it can look up the evidence and arguments for themselves, and those that have not or will not look into the evidence should remain silent until they have. Also, those that believe the theory, according to their integrity, should also go on to tell their kids that they evolved out of fungus, or worms, or whatever it is in the ocean. Maybe a cheery spin can be put on it in the modern humanistic fashion.

necessities and God for 20 years, I would like to know what else he would need for happiness. What *else* in addition to God would be required for him to feel alright? Even someone who is normally insistent that the creator alone is sufficient for us, would have a list of things that the guy in solitary would also have to have in order to be doing okay. But to say that the guy in solitary confinement would be unhappy, would be saying, in short, "God is not enough. To be happy, we need more than just God."

Nevertheless, some people would still claim that a person who had sufficient faith, or who had some other quality, *would* be happy in a cell for 20 years. And that thought actually would be correct. A creature designed to be content solely in God *would* be happy. But that is most certainly *not* the homo sapien. It's useful to remember for practical purposes and for expectations in life that God made all the animals, and that he made man. Or, it might be better to say, God made all the animals, and man was one of them. Unlike the others, it seems, he made homo sapiens capable of a relationship with him, and with spiritual life. But nobody should forget that the homo sapien is still an animal. And these thoughts now begin to get at the best answer that I know of for happiness in life, and that I doubt I will ever change my mind about in my lifetime here.

The best answer

Our species *is* a species, and there aren't many creatures that do not have a particular set of things they need in order to be happy. Not many species at all do well without contact with others of their kind, for example. They might start pulling feathers, chewing on their feet, or licking their fur until they wear a hole in it and have to wear a dog-from-space collar. Some species will actually die without being around their fellows. Or, if an animal of almost any type is put in a little cage, they won't be doing too well because they do not have what they *need* to be happy. Put *man* in a cage with nothing to do, without contact with others of his kind, and he won't be doing so well either. God doesn't "cure" the nature he gave the man-creature when one of them accepts God as his or her God so that the connection is all he needs—at least, obviously not in this world.

There are Christian hymns and songs with words like, "...you are my all in all...I need nothing but you...etc." but they aren't true. It would be nice if he was our all in all and we needed nothing but him, and he, being God, could do that easily, but he normally does not, and that is also obvious. It doesn't take boldness or any moral quality to realize it; only a rational mind and a willingness to accept the obvious. If we don't have food and water, we'll die in a most unpleasant way; if we don't have contact with others we'll be miserable; if we don't have a change of scenery or don't get to move around regularly we'll be unhappy; if we have a mental problem, we'll be unhappy; if we have some major birth defect so that we are never really accepted or at ease around our fellows, we'll be unhappy. And all of these things will be true whether we have God or not. Yet again, the only exception will be if the maker takes miraculous action. But history and experience show that he rarely does. The list could go on quite a bit further for things that will spoil our good time here, and just from observation it seems that we are designed to find what we need to be happy in God first, but not in him alone.

The truth is that the wildabeast needs grass and a place to run, and the homo sapien needs something different and mindless to do part of the time, for one thing. The wildabeast and frogs, dogs and lizards probably can't have a conscious relationship with God at all. All they need is food, running or jumping room, a warm rock to lie on, and other things according to how they are made. Man-beast can know God consciously, though, and he needs more than land to walk and food to eat. He needs God too, badly, but like the other animals, there are other things we need as well, and these are by no means limited to physical needs. What we want is a smorgasbord of stuff in order to feel alright. *That* is the situation, and that is part of the best answer to how we can be happy.

Senseless and unthinking distraction is part of our food, for example. We need to know a God who loves us, to be connected to people, a wife or husband to share things with, something exciting to do occasionally, decent food, dirt to roll in and a bone to chew on for my friend Mark, several cats to dress up like little people and to have tea parties with for my friend Rob, enough rest, enough distraction, etc. Hume said, "it seems, then, that nature has pointed out a mixed kind of life as most suitable to the human race, and secretly admonished them to allow none of these biases to *draw* too much, so as to incapacitate them for other occupations and entertainments."[151] That's about right. If any one of these things is removed, it's not so likely at all that some other thing is going to grow to fill the hole. That's the simple truth, despite how spiritual any of us might be.

Conclusion

Concluding now, I should say that I do not believe that happiness is impossible or that it's useless or selfish to try. There is almost no objective in life more noble or intimidating than to seek genuine freedom and fulfillment in your own heart. And things like human approval or wealth are not what any human being really wants. People will pursue things like that because they're too scared to face what's really lacking.

New or tangential ideas aren't recommended at the end of any discussion, but I'll still add here that if an effort is ever going to be made at real happiness, *now* is the time for it. Some people who make no effort at it tell themselves that what they're doing is sacrificing for others. Some parents, for example, ignore their own souls and tell themselves that they're doing it for their kids when, in

---

[151] Hume, *Enquiry*, section I, ~ p 4.

reality, what they're doing is passing the buck onto the next generation because they're too scared to dare for themselves. Didn't their parents work so that *they* could have a chance at real life? Or the wars we've fought in the past—those guys suffered and faced terrifying threats and overcame them so that *we, now*, could pursue real life. If everybody keeps "sacrificing" and passing it on down the line, who is supposed to ever live the life that keeps being prepared for? What future generation off in the distant perfect world we've made is finally going to be able to be happy? If an attempt is going to be made, now is the time for it, and the best hope is in God.[152]

We should seek real happiness, then, but in the end we should also remember the sad truth that it's unlikely we will ever feel complete as a normal condition in this world, no matter what we do. Even if outside circumstances are perfect, there are still some major problems in each of us. God seems to have designed people to need a variety of things to be happy, and anyone can fill in the pie chart of what we need in the most reverent or practical way possible, and we can do everything right in life, but each of us will still feel the holes and defects that are in us, to some degree. There *is* happiness in God beyond our capacity to bear or contain, and nowhere else, but there isn't much chance we will grasp it in this life, outside of a few precious moments.

---

[152] I won't get into more biblical teaching here, but the christian texts also say that there is only one way to establish a relationship with him.

Now we know that if the earthly tent we live in is destroyed, we have a building from God, an eternal house in heaven, not built by human hands. Meanwhile we groan, longing to be clothed with our heavenly dwelling, because when we are clothed, we will not be found naked. For while we are in this tent, we groan and are burdened, because we do not wish to be unclothed but to be clothed with our heavenly dwelling, so that what is mortal may be swallowed up by life
(2 Corinthians 5:1-4).

Conclusion of My Life, and of Fulfillment

I'll finish by concluding my own story, in the context of my experience with happiness. Summarizing things with this focus helps to frame a final conclusion for fulfillment in this world, and it helps to describe how I got to the point of living as I do now—in case anyone might care to know.

As a child life was great aside from some boredom, but by the time I was about eight things were not as great because my conscience got to me and I had to start living with myself as not a complete innocent. From thirteen to fifteen things were terrible and I had actually thought that I would have been better off dead. After that time passed life was better for a while until my third year of high school, at which time I wanted to either overcome everything that had ever plagued me, or come to an end of the whole thing right there.

It was at that time that my particular experience with happiness became unique and worth telling. I had the simple goal of trying to feel alright and to be free, like everyone does, but for me conditions combined in a way that made me unusually determined. Content people are content, and someone who is comfortable and having a good time doesn't have much to strive for. Pain, on the other hand, is quite a good stimulant to action. People that are not having such a good time are driven to seek something—some kind of salve and some kind of cure—and I was most fortunate in having had the heck kicked out of me over many years in order to motivate me to do that, and to push me to be willing to do whatever I had to.

I had the human drive for fulfillment to an inordinate degree, and for a couple months after I'd believed in Christ, I had achieved that ultimate goal! I'd actually arrived at happiness and peace—the objective for any human being, but the one that essentially no one ever gets to. It was the pinnacle of my life, and it worked, and it was real. But then I went back to my old life and lost it all.

When I came to my senses after only a couple months I tried to get it back, with my absolute best effort. For a long time afterwards I was intent on sorting things out, regaining what I'd lost, and getting back to that place again. For a long time I wouldn't let myself rest or be diverted, but I remained in something like a state of mourning; like an observance or vigil for an issue that had to be resolved. It was a lot of years that this effort went on, as if I was on campaign and it was no time for enjoyment. I kept my eyes on where I was compared to where I had been, in order to remember it, since things that are ignored are not solved.

Spiritual issues and religious beliefs were involved heavily in this for me, but my situation wasn't limited to that. The human quest for happiness was the issue as well, and this is part of why describing my particular experience in this context is worthwhile. My case is not one that has no relation to others and to the common problem of the race. We all have some recognition that we are not where we should be, as if we've fallen from where we belong and we are desperate to get there again—like the explorer from a tale who found a hidden land where happiness was a reality, but then left for some reason and could never find his way back again. That allegory for the human race is especially true for me, and my life became the equivalent of spending all I had on equipment for the search: crossing deserts, sleeping in the open on the ground for years, and generally suffering on a trek to find the way back again to that place I'd been, rather than giving up and accepting that I would never be able to.

I had known since I was a teenager that happiness, or the real obstacle to it, rather, lies within ourselves. That knowledge was why I lived in a lonely room out in the country instead of living in town for five years while I worked at a Naval base that was basically a male barracks. It's part of why I didn't own a television for 10 years, didn't watch movies, didn't have video games, company, or anything else. Knowing that the real obstacle was within me was the reason that I have or have not done a lot of things over the years.[153] I avoided distraction and the common enjoyments of human beings and I stared into the dark, hoping that I might cut away one more set of vines and see the break in the rock wall that I had left through years before. I hoped that I would find the trail that led back to that place where things were as they should be—where I knew God was with me and my faith was working, and where I knew fulfillment. I maintained ascetic habits like these because of my determination to get things right within myself. It was all part of the vigil and the observance for the issue that had not been resolved, but that had to be.

Whatever it took, *that* was what I was going to do.

> You are a youth no longer, you are now a full-grown man. If now you are careless and indolent and are always putting off, fixing one day after another as the limit when you mean to begin attending to yourself, then, living or dying, you will make no progress but will continue unawares in ignorance. Therefore make up your mind before it is too late to live as one who is mature and proficient, and let all that seems best to you be a law that you cannot transgress. And if you encounter anything troublesome or pleasant or glorious or inglorious, remember that the hour of struggle is come, the Olympic contest is here and you may put off no longer, and

---

[153] Although, in truth, even if I had found some distraction, I would have felt just the same unrest and discontent and anxiety if I had been carving model planes or pasting stamps in my collection or whatever else people use to pass the time.

> that one day and one action determines whether the progress you have achieved is lost or maintained.[154]

That was Epictetus, which I read only recently, but which I believed since I was a teenager, absolutely. If you do not do what you need to now, you probably never will, and no one will take your place. *Whatever it takes* or whatever it means, you had better get it done or you will continue living as you are now and then you'll die as you are now.

Along the same lines, I kept a couple things in mind that Jesus said: "From the time of John the Baptist until now, the kingdom of heaven suffers violence, and violent men take it by force." And, "Seek and you will find; knock and the door will be opened to you." And I kept in mind that the woman with the bleeding problem pushed her *own* way through the crowd to touch Jesus. If *you* seek *you* will find. If you don't find what it takes to reach out and take it, then you are the one who will not have, and you'll live a scared, distracted life, and die a sorry old man.

People go their whole lives with something wrong, but won't take the boldness to face it, and they'll die that way because they didn't have the guts to do what needed to be done. I had told myself for a long time that I would not do that, and I had worked very hard to be the person who would do what was called for, no matter what, etc., (although, after my initial success, I turned out to be just a poor unhappy bastard). But I *was* serious—there was no doubt about that—and I was determined to do whatever I had to do to get back to a place where things were right. I'd been completely committed once before as a teenager to achieve something, and my goal had been reached then after a monumental effort.

However,

---

[154] Epictetus, *Manual*, 51.

I had tried my best since that life transforming event to overcome again, in the same way as far as I could, for years, and I'd had much different results. Misery and failure. Those were my results. I had always felt *horrible*. Worse, in fact, in direct proportion to how hard I tried. After a lot of years of effort, discipline, difficulty and pain, the trek had gotten me nowhere and the vigil had ended up being worthless.

A new phase started when I was 25, though. I finally became angry about what had happened to me and at the way things had been, and I sat looking back at those facts, facing the great discontent, and reviewing the great horsecrap that life had been for a lot of years, *and* that it looked like it would continue being until I died. I knew very well what things had been for me for a long time, and I kept firmly in mind just how bad all of those years had been and how I had been destroyed. It made me deeply angry, and I knew then, after I'd finally taken an honest look at it all, that nothing would ever change unless I went to further lengths to change it, and unless I did whatever it took.

Enough time spent in the way I spent my time then will build resolve. And after my anger shifted away from God to rest on my situation, a change in strategy and a more determined and final form of action evolved in my mind. I said chapters back that a drastic plan had taken root in my mind during those years, but I didn't describe what it was.

The plan

My foremost idea was to go into the woods without much of anything, and not to come back out until God had answered me or until I had found out what was wrong and what I could do. I was indignant; from the outside all the way in, and had suffered about as much as would be possible without actually being afflicted physically. And if God could not at least answer me, then he could watch me starve. I had tried everything else for a lot of years and it seemed to be time to do something that was guaranteed to have results one way or another.

As it happens, the mathematician friend of mine from Wyoming told me once, back during those years after I had decided on a plan, that when he was fifteen he had walked up on top of a windswept mountain and had stayed there without food for three days. Excuse my language, but there are two main things required to do something like that: balls, and determination to get what you want. There may be some other things involved also, like stupidity, but being very smart and wise is not what keeps the vast majority of people from ever doing anything similar in their lives. Fear, complacency, and lack of any kind of resolve is the reason for that.[155] After my friend told me the story, I guessed that he had read about Native Americans doing things like the mountaintop fasts trying to experience some kind of vision, and he said that was exactly what it had been about. His outing was not too far off from what I was readying myself for, but my goal was different and was more serious. God was going to answer me, or I was going to die out there.

In part, it was going to be like taking myself hostage. I'd had enough, God hadn't done anything to help me, and I just wasn't going to participate anymore. If he cared, he could do something, or the hostage would die.[156] I was going to do something that would be guaranteed to make it all give.

---

[155] The dominant thought and instinct for most of us is to protect our precious lives, no matter what, and to live as long as humanly possible. Risk doesn't factor in.

[156] That is the most accurate analogy for it. But it was also partly going to be like taking a shot at a life. I'd said that the gap between my state and a state of any kind of peace or happiness had become very distinct, almost like something I could see, and something was going to be the target of all the feelings that had finally gotten out. I have no desire to appear ostentatious by including the following comparison, and I hesitated to even put it in a footnote, but there truly was a similarity too strong to omit mention of: "[Ahab] at last came to identify with him [the whale], not only all his bodily woes, but all his intellectual and spiritual exasperations. The White Whale swam before him as the monomaniac incarnation of all those malicious agencies which some deep men feel eating in them, till they are left living on with half a heart and half a lung...all the subtle

Since I've been a Christian I have always had some very close friends that I've talked to about what's going on — about almost everything — but this plan was one thing I made sure not to tell anyone about, ever (adhering to the approach it seems that everyone who is going to do something that may be suicidal follows instinctually). Even when Carlos described the thing that he'd done, I didn't mention a word of what I had in mind, and I remember bottling it up as we walked through the parking lot that day. The reason specifically that I told no one, and that other people with similar ideas don't tell anyone, is that fear and desire for comfort are already hard enough to overcome without other people trying to dissuade you so that your resolve finally breaks. I didn't speak of what I had in mind to do until many years later, and if it was still my plan, or if I thought that it ever would be again in the future, I would not be talking about it now.

I was most determined to change something or be finished when I was living down in Blacksburg at school, but I knew that I couldn't follow through with it at that time. I remember one day, for example, not having eaten for a few meals and not wanting to eat. I would have taken my shot right then if I could have, but as I sat in the living room, angry and having had more than enough of the life I had been in for so many years, I reasoned with myself that if I went ahead any further with this plan then, there was no way I would be able to handle my classes and graduate. I said gently to myself, as to some angry animal, that I would have to treat myself decently or I wouldn't be able to finish. So I ate something and kept on, putting it on hold for the future. If it hadn't been for school I just might be a skeleton in the woods right now…or, I might have encountered God in some way or found out something that would have once again changed the rest of my life.

---

demonisms of life and thought; all evil, to crazy Ahab, were visibly personified, and made practically assailable in Moby Dick. He piled upon the whale's white hump the sum of all the general rage and hate felt by his whole race from Adam down" *Moby Dick*, chapter 41.

I graduated, though, and got a job, and had to pay my loans off. I don't remember exactly what kept me from heading for a remote spot in the woods as soon as I finished the degree. Maybe it was lack of the commitment to actually do it after all, but I don't think so. There was never a time I thought about it and was ready to depart, but became too scared or decided it was crazy. During those first several years as an engineer I still had this plan in my mind to follow, and still never told anyone a word about it. I was definitely still going to do something final, and was just biding my time. I remember that whenever personal career goals and objectives came up at work, that we were supposed to describe and take very seriously, it meant nothing to me because I might not be long for this world. Also, before I even finished school I had decided that I would only work in engineering long enough to pay my loans off, then would leave, in order to settle things that mattered and that were the real mountains in life, although I didn't know exactly how I would do it. The possibility of taking myself hostage or otherwise forcing an end to the situation of being alive in a corrupted, discontented, unhappy, unfulfilled, angry, anxious, uncertain life, was still very much in mind.

By the end of my second year at work my plan had changed somewhat since I had decided to write down what I'd experienced in life and the things I had figured out. I would get that done, no matter what, and that goal became the most important thing to me almost as soon as I had decided on it.

So, I never did take myself hostage trying force some kind of resolution. I'm pretty sure I'd had enough pain and had developed enough determination that I would have gone and done it if circumstances had been slightly different. And I am sure that I would have at least walked out and not eaten for days. I couldn't say where I might have been by the end of the first five days if I had gone; possibly even more determined not to give up and go back to the same junk, knowing that if I did, it would last the rest of my life.

I can't tell what other people might think of this—if it might seem like bluster—and I don't have much evidence other than my own word to show that it's not phony garbage. I would not want that to be thought of any of these chapters, so I will point out a couple things that I can as evidence that it is genuine: I volunteered to work in Iraq for several months, because I wanted to see it. I have a long scar on the back of my rib cage from a dare to myself when I was 19 involving a gorge and a jump, which was pointless, but was also serious and pretty frightening also. Several times in situations where a dangerous type of person or people were being offensive to everyone around them in restaurants and other places, I have been the one to confront them, when no one else would. (And I might be scared in things. I might be scared to death, and weakness might start gripping my throat, but I will be darned if I will sit and not take action in life. I will usually force myself to do what I should.)

And, as a last example, I'll mention that I left a career job with the kind of pay and conditions that no one leaves. And I didn't leave for another position as a contractor making more money. I left for making no money at all; for three years now, with $45,000 in student loans still, in order to do something that I was convicted that I should. I sold my car, cashed out my retirement, etc. A lot of people told me how dangerous what I was doing was and how I shouldn't have done it for one reason or another. But I hope I will never forget what I saw, and what I was in 1996, and I hope that I will never go from having been that person, to being a frightened little man too scared to do what I think I should in life. So help me God.

As I said, there was never a moment that I considered acting on my plan but then definitively changed my mind about it. Things just shifted over time. One large factor in this shift was that I began to appreciate, only in the last couple years, how broken human beings all really are, and always will be. *All* of us. I began to appreciate that we will probably never get over our discontent, or ever really be fulfilled, regardless of whether we're trying or not. I wrote all of these conclusions in earlier chapter.

For many years I knew that fleeing to distractions because of an inability to sit in peace was weak, and that it showed that the individual wasn't willing to face what he needed to. I was right. That is true for a lot of people a lot of the time. But it's also true that the human being needs some distraction just like a parrot needs some toys in his cage to play with. I thought also that all that somebody should need in order to be content is God, and that having to be around other people frequently was a weakness demonstrating that you weren't able to face yourself. I was right there also. A lot of people seek company constantly because they won't face themselves, and they're terrified of silence. But it isn't true across the board, in all situations. We were born with some big empty spaces in us, and company can help to fill one of them a little bit. Nothing else is going to replace that. And that same condition of empty spaces inside us, and specific matches for them, that have no substitute, is true for all of the other things that we need to be happy as well—nothing else will do.

It took me a long time to learn these things and it took a long time to learn that discontent and an inability to sit in peace is also part of the human condition, and that it's very unlikely that it will ever be overcome completely. I also finally realized how special the time I experienced in 1996 was, and that it is something that is probably never to be regained…ever…no matter how hard I try or what I do. Thank goodness I finally concluded that. A lot of what had driven me over all those years to reject the life of unfulfillment was that I had in fact experienced genuine victory when I had first encountered God. I had actually *been there*! I had been to that place and lived there, so I thought that it all should be possible again permanently.

As I learned later, though, it's possible, but it is very unlikely. I learned that not being there does mean that something is seriously wrong, but it doesn't mean I have to keep on the trek at all costs, forsaking everything else. Something is seriously wrong, but that's part of our condition in this life and it will never be cured here. Realizing these things probably had the biggest part in changing my plan of forcing God to act, or of starving, and had the biggest part in ending the vigil.

I'll also mention that if I had done what I had planned to, God may very well have spoken, and the colossal hurdle—common to all of us in a way—might have been overcome, or at least been answered; because of a determination to really bang on the door. But I think it's equally likely that God would have watched me die. He has watched a lot of things happen in this world.

It would have made a very interesting story if I'd done it and survived to tell about it, but I also want to mention that hopefully I won't be responsible for putting the idea into a bunch of kids who'll go out and starve in the woods. I wouldn't exactly recommend it to anyone, for the same reason that I learned—that we will *never* overcome our problems or obstacles to fulfillment completely, unless we can change ourselves to be some other type of creation than we were born as.

In addition to that, I don't think God has usually responded as we would like to attempts to force him to act.

> "To what, then, can I compare the people of this generation? What are they like? They are like children sitting in the marketplace and calling out to each other:
>
>> 'We played the flute for you,
>> And you did not dance;
>> we sang a dirge,
>> and you did not cry'" (Luke 7:31-33).

No one should probably ever expect God to dance to their tune, or let his arm be twisted by us. He is very, very far above us, and the word majesty means something when it's spoken of him.

In the end, I do still respect the nobility of doing *what, ever, it, takes*, to overcome something, to grab a hold of God, and to get closer to him. He is the wellspring of all life and of every good thing, and there is no higher pursuit.

Was there ever an answer?

I had finished this chapter right here before, but I felt like I needed to go back and include a little more to answer the question of what my problem was over all those years; and that still is my problem and probably always will be.

For about fourteen years I asked myself ten-thousand times, "what's wrong, and why can't I get back to where I was?" And the most likely answer, which I am pretty sure of, is that I have never been able to recover the faith I had at first.

As David Hume said, and as we all know, you can tell when you believe something or doubt something because it produces corresponding feelings in you. And over all those years that I was trying, and doing everything that I could, I could feel that I didn't have the same faith. It was unmistakable. This Christianity that I had wasn't working anymore and I doubted the whole thing constantly—although I made the best effort that I possibly could not to ever doubt it.

I personally have a hindrance to being able to believe or to trust; as I had mentioned chapters back. For the first couple months in 1996 I was able to get past that, but after my decision to abandon my new life, I have never been able to take that step of trust again. And so I have never had those same feelings that accompany a genuine working faith. There is a verse where Paul instructs his pupil Timothy to hold tight to his "faith and a good conscience. For by rejecting this, some have made shipwreck of their faith" (1 Tim. 1:19). I apparently did that. And it's hard to put a ship back together that has been wrecked.

Some years ago, though, I learned that I cannot fix this, and I gave up on trying. I realized that if it's going to be resolved, God is going to have to do it. So it's not my problem anymore. And, like I mentioned previously, I learned at about age 28, that salvation is forever, even if your faith is wrecked and you care barely tell that you believe it any more. If God has given someone eternal life, it's eternal, and if he has forgiven all your sins, he has forgiven all your sins. Eternal life that you can lose isn't eternal, by definition, and if any of your sins are brought up again and put on your account, then they weren't forgiven.

I also learned something else at about age 32 after I had resigned from my job: that *I am human*. And that has meant a lot. I realized that the problems that are common to our species are basically never going to be overcome. Not by me and not by anyone else.

And I realized another naïve assumption that I had held. I thought for years that everyone who believes in Christ has that same kind of certainty that I had at first, and that, therefore, something was deeply and especially wrong with me since I no longer had it. That wasn't true at all. Most other Christians probably do, in fact, have more faith than I do, but nobody is truly certain, and probably very, very few people approach the kind of confidence and faith that I had at the beginning. I didn't know it at the time, but I had quite a faith then.

So that's my best conclusion on what caused me so much grief for so many years, and that continues to be a major challenge for me. It had always been faith. God never did speak to me about what the problem was, and what was wrong that devastated my psyche and my youth. But that is my best answer—a lack of faith, combined with my penchant for embracing the worst possibilities and expecting unrealistic things from myself—and I'm pretty sure that it's right.

I still question what I'm going to do for the rest of my time here. I realized about a year ago that I had never even thought of the possibility of having to live for more than a couple years after leaving my first job, and that I had never even thought about any life beyond that. Almost the entire screen was blank. There was not a single plan, dream, or idea. As introspective as I am, this was strange, and I realized that the reason for it was that I had accepted for a long time that my life would end about right now — age thirty four. The trek was going to be successful, or I wasn't going to be coming back from it. I know now, though, that I will probably never force that change or die in a torrent of blood and spray trying to overcome, and reach fulfillment. ...More's the pity. I'll probably never find my way back to the place I was at before. I honestly believe that this is the way I will remain until this life is done. There are things that people cannot do, even within themselves.

But I would still not give up completely on possibilities, because God does exist and he can do things that we can't. In addition to all the trouble I've experienced, I've learned that one as well, and I can describe one event that demonstrates it.

I'll mention, as background for this example, that my parents are conservative in their speech and behavior and that I learned the example of reserve from my father, like he learned from his father, who captained a naval destroyer, if that gives some idea. I have usually avoided attention in my life. And I've been known since elementary school as being the stoical one who makes no expression. I'm still reserved today, and I was even more so when I was eighteen when this event happened. And, given the contrast of this incident with my nature and background, it still serves as a good reminder for me.

A couple weeks after first starting college I got a ride out to a particular church for the first time, and at the beginning of service that day, as soon as they started playing music, I found myself on my knees right at the pew I was sitting at while everyone else was standing up appropriately.¹⁵⁷ It never went through my mind, "I think I'll kneel down here between these pews," and it never even occurred to me to worry about anyone looking at me or to wonder what anyone thought of it, or if I should do it. As conscious as I am of myself and my surroundings, and considerate of my actions, just that fact in itself would be impossible through any effort I could make.

More importantly, though, while I was down there I was way off in another place, and I saw myself at God's feet. He was sitting and I was kneeling, and the whole world was out of sight and out of mind. In addition to being reserved, I also learned a great distrust for emotions or for the word *love*, very early on, but kneeling on the floor there that day I could feel God's love for me and I never wanted to come back to this world. I remember having no sense of time, but I was down there for that whole segment of service, because I got up and sat back on the pew when everyone else sat down again.

Nothing quite like that has ever happened to me again, and not a single part of it was my doing. But God is able to do what he is pleased to, and we might never guess what that might be. I have had a number of other experiences over the years that obviously were his action as well but, along with one other, that was the most powerful and meaningful one; sixteen years ago.

A final example that illustrates the possibilities for us even while we still remain in this world is from John Wesley's journal. Wesley described a man named John Downes whom he regarded as like "a Methodist Isaac Newton" because of his outstanding abilities.¹⁵⁸ Wesley said of Downes:

---

[157] This happened to be a place where people were aware that God can act still in this world, so it didn't seem too strange to them, and they were aware of what might have happened to me.

[158] Wesley says that once when Downes was a child, his father sent him to get a clock fixed. Downes watched the clockmaker work while he was there, built the tools he had

> For several months past, he had far deeper communion with God, than ever he had had in his life; and for some days he had been frequently saying, "I am so happy, that I scarce know how to live. I enjoy such fellowship with God, as I thought could not be had on this side heaven." And having now finished his course of fifty-two years, after a long conflict with pain, sickness, and poverty, he gloriously rested from his labours, and entered into the joy of his Lord.[159]

A lot more of the language in older days, I think, was trumpet blowing, and there were more attempts made by certain groups and individuals—like John Wesley—to force everything to fit ideals of what was supposed to happen. But I do believe the accuracy of that entry above, and I don't think that John Downes reached that place of being "so happy that he scarce knew how to live" by his own efforts. Somebody's conscience would have to be clear to get to that condition, and he would have to be doing what he should be, but in the end God is the one who gives life to things.

Fulfillment might always be a little bit out of reach for us here, but there is always the possibility that God may take action to do something inside us that we just can't do, if we make an effort to be near to him. There is always the hope of that, no matter what our circumstances may be.

> *"I seek you with all my heart"* (Psalm 119:10).

> *"You will seek me and find me when you seek me with all your heart"* (Jeremiah 29:13).

---

seen there when he got home, then built a clock that kept time as well as any other in the town.

[159] John Wesley's Journal, Monday October 31, 1774.

The Best Answer

I hope not to have bored anyone with anything I've written. I personally would not do well as a manager because I can barely stand listening to uninteresting talk in groups. I think my experience is an engaging tale, though, so I'll only use the word "I" a few more times and be finished.

I don't know how things would have gone if I hadn't messed everything up in the summer of 1996. The whole experience, though, before and after, has helped to make me capable of writing all this. If it hadn't happened, maybe I would not have been able to compose something valuable, as I believe this to be. Similarly, if Martin Luther had been a cheerful happy-go-lucky man through all his years, he probably wouldn't have ever had enough and resolved that his life as a monk was terrible and that he wasn't going to do it anymore. If he was happy he might have never actually read the Bible to see that forgiveness is a gift. Even after he discovered this, though, his life and writings certainly still did not convey a sense of a cheerful guy enjoying Christian life.

I do not want to give the impression that the Christian life is a concentration camp, though. Most Christians have a much better time than I have. Most that I have known have been the happiest people I've encountered, and they've always had more hope than other people in the world, as is only logical that they should. The reason it has been as it has been for me might be that it was ordained that way for a particular purpose after all. I think that the vast majority of all that happens in this world is just what happens and that there is no meaning or reason for it other than most senseless coincidence. That is not a pleasant thing to believe but it's what I think is true. However, some things are God's doing. He might give or withhold or even inflict in order to motivate, but no one would usually be able to discern those actions for certain, much less be able to tell God that he's wrong.

The past is mostly past, but whatever I might be doing to pay for fuel for my stomach for the remainder of my years here, I will also probably always keep telling myself one thing that I was told myself two and a half years ago. The slogan of the Boy Scouts is "be prepared" but this other phrase would be my slogan, if I had one, since the time I heard it. I was visiting a friend in southwest Virginia three years ago and had been set off by some bad news I'd gotten. On that day the world looked almost as dark as it ever has, and I really didn't want to be in it anymore. I just could not see how or why everyone could try to cling to life here so desperately, with the way this place is and how our experience is in it. I have hardly ever been so down, which, for me, is really saying something. But that night as I slept I heard the words, "I left you here to tell people" then I immediately woke up.

God has only spoken directly to me a handful of times in my life, and that was one of them, and it made perfect sense to me. Actually it is the only thing that would make sense. He didn't say, "no, you're wrong, the world is nice" or "I left you here for practice living in a land of insanity and pain." I should not have needed anything but a rational mind to realize why anyone would still be on this earth, given what the Bible says, but I will never forget those words and the circumstances that surrounded them. The main purpose for any Christian in still being here is to work so that more people hear the gospel; not to be happy, although we should all try for that also. And one thing this means is that part of any Christian's job here is simply to *endure*, whether things are good or bad.

My main purpose all along in writing this book was to discharge some of the responsibility that was given to me July 4, 1996—to tell people that Jesus Christ came "to give his life as a ransom for many" and that he offers forgiveness and eternal life to anyone who asks.

This is the gospel:

The Bible has both bad and good news. There is bad news because every human being has done some ugly things, and there will be judgment for them. Without forgiveness we will be punished. For example, Jesus spoke of some supposedly religious people that "devour widows' houses and for a show make lengthy prayers," and said that "such men will be punished most severely" (Luke 20:47). He doesn't miss things. Most people are just trying to live and be happy the best they can, but we are all still guilty and we are all in very serious trouble on our own. As it says, "There is not a righteous man on earth who does what is right and never sins" (Eccl. 7:20).

I will say that I don't *want* to believe that there is punishment. It has just about torn the heart right out of me over these years and it still colors this entire world for me. But I'm not going to bury my head or start lying to anyone. A whole lot of people want to believe in Jesus as God, but they don't want to believe in him as savior because that would mean that we all *need* a savior. The majority of what are supposed to be churches, though, do that exact thing. If you go to a service, by the way, or to any other nominally Christian group, but never hear or see the message that we need salvation, and that it's through faith in Christ, and no other way, you should go somewhere else.

The bad news, then, is that there is a judgement at the end, and punishment for what we've done wrong. But the good news is that whoever believes in Jesus Christ will be forgiven completely and made perfectly clean, as if he or she had never done anything wrong. Both the bad and good news is in each of these verses:

> "If you do not believe that I am the one I claim to be, you will indeed die in your sins" (John 8:24).

> "Whoever believes in the Son has eternal life, but whoever rejects the Son will not see life, for God's wrath remains on him" (John 3:36).

> "Just as man is destined to die once, and after that to face judgment, so Christ was sacrificed once to take away the sins of many people" (Hebrews 9:28).

> "I tell you the truth, whoever hears my word and believes him who sent me has eternal life and will not be condemned; he has crossed over from death to life" (John 5:24).

> "The Son of Man did not come to be served, but to serve, and to give his life as a ransom for many" (Matthew 20:28).

God had ordered the Jews in ancient times to offer sacrifices. The idea was that the sins of the people would be transferred to the animal to be sacrificed, and that it would die for the peoples' offenses instead of the people dying for them. The reason for all these sacrifices was to serve as a symbol so that Christ's actions could be understood better when he came. Jesus himself was the sacrifice and, unlike bulls, goats, and sheep, his sacrifice was able to remove sins:

"He is the atoning sacrifice for our sins, and not only for ours but also for the sins of the whole world" (1 John 2:2).

"He loved us and sent his Son as an atoning sacrifice for our sins" (1 John 4:10).

Unlike the other high priests, he does not need to offer sacrifices day after day, first for his own sins, and then for the sins of the people. He sacrificed for their sins once for all when he offered himself" (Hebrews 7:27).

That is good news. Christ's sacrifice was effective and can remove all sins so that we can be perfectly clean and enter God's presence (heaven). All that's necessary to receive this forgiveness, and to receive a new life, is faith in Jesus Christ. But an individual has to be willing to repent—which means a willingness to accept God as God of his or her life and not only as a hobby or cultural practice. Faith is all that's necessary for salvation, but there can't be genuine faith without repentance. Those who "believe" in Jesus Christ but do exactly as they have always done and exactly as they please, have never accepted him as their God. Repentance is necessary:

He told them, 'This is what is written: The Messiah will suffer and rise from the dead on the third day, and repentance for the forgiveness of sins will be preached in his name to all nations, beginning at Jerusalem. You are witnesses of these things' (Luke 24:38).

"But unless you repent, you too will all perish" (Luke 13:5).

After John was put in prison, Jesus went into Galilee, proclaiming the good news of God. 'The time has come,' he said. 'The kingdom of God has come near. Repent and believe the good news!' (Mark 1:14-15).

Again, salvation or being a Christian doesn't come by being good. It's by faith. But genuine faith is connected to repentance and there can't be one without the other. I can understand very well if a person has trouble believing, or does not believe—that should be quite clear from what I've written before—but there's also a good question to be asked, which is that, if you *knew* the Bible was true, would you accept God as God of your life? If the answer is "no" then it doesn't make much difference if you kind of believe it or not.

There is a heaven:

Do not let your hearts be troubled. Trust in God; trust also in me. In my Father's house are many rooms; if it were not so, I would have told you. I am going there to prepare a place for you. And if I go and prepare a place for you, I will come back and take you to be with me that you also may be where I am (John 14:1-3).

Whoever receives him will have a restored relationship with him. God went to the most extreme lengths to make this possible because he cares about us and he created us exactly for relationship with him.

"You are all children of God through faith in Christ Jesus" (Gal 3:26).

"Here I am! I stand at the door and knock. If anyone hears my voice and opens the door, I will come in and eat with him, and he with me" (Revelation 3:20).

"Gospel" means "good news," and this is why. According to the Bible, again, whoever decides to believe and accept Jesus Christ as their God will have a new life, complete forgiveness, and the promise of heaven. No priest, church building, or holy water is needed. It's between you and God and you can get it settled today. And you don't have to wonder if God wants *you* or will accept *you*. He already said that he "wants all people to be saved, and to come to a knowledge of the truth" (1 Tim. 2:4).

A prayer helps. Ask God to forgive you, and say that you believe in Jesus Christ. Again, Jesus himself said, "whoever believes has eternal life" (John 6:47). If you've decided you want him to be your savior, then it's yours, and you should be baptized. Baptism is a powerful symbol to declare that the old life is gone for good, the new life has come, and that you are now associated with Jesus Christ.

I hope that everyone reading this will accept the same God who saved me — perfect in righteousness, deserving of all honor, but still stooping down to rescue us and to allow us to know him.

*"Let my mouth be filled with thy praise
and with thy honour all the day."*

(Psalm 71:8)

www.ingramcontent.com/pod-product-compliance
Lightning Source LLC
Chambersburg PA
CBHW030434010526
44118CB00011B/627